D1109205

3 1215 00010 7190

NATIONAL ANTHEMS OF THE WORLD

[Shaw, Martin Fallas]

NATIONAL ANTHEMS of the WORLD

Edited by

T. M. CARTLEDGE and W. L. REED
MARTIN SHAW and HENRY COLEMAN

ARCO PUBLISHING COMPANY, INC.
New York

Published 1978 by Arco Publishing Company, Inc.
219 Park Avenue South, New York, N.Y. 10003

Printed in Great Britain

Library of Congress Cataloging in Publication Data

Shaw, Martin Fallas, 1875-1958.
National anthems of the world.

Principally for voice and piano; words in English or in the original languages, with English translation.
1. National songs. I. Coleman, Henry, 1888-1965, joint ed. II. Cartledge, T. M., joint ed. III. Title.
M1627.S55N33 1978 784.7'19 78-231
ISBN 0-668-04496-9

CONTENTS

Publisher's Preface and Acknowledgements

Since the last edition of this book a number of countries have achieved independence, along with a new national anthem; others have revised their anthems for various reasons. We are able to incorporate new anthems for Mozambique, Papua New Guinea, Guinea-Bissau and Transkei; we also include the anthems for the Yemen Arab Republic, the United Arab Emirates and the State Anthems for all thirteen states of Malaysia. A vocal line has been added for Rhodesia, and we have made amendments where either words have been altered or the name of the country has changed.

Countries which are the dependent territories of other countries principally use the national anthem of the "mother country". Where a country has in addition its own national song which is used on important occasions this is also given; the songs of the Cayman Islands and Belize have been added.

Some anthems are now obsolete in that they are not officially authorised by the State; they are included, however, not to be abrasive politically, but to provide a historical record for expatriot communities.

Every effort has been made to make this edition as up to date as possible and any necessary minor amendments have been incorporated. Inevitably, however, there are several anthems for which we have been unable to obtain either music, words or both, despite much research.

For the new anthems we are indebted to the Embassies and their staffs who have supplied much of the information and to the Royal Marines School of Music, for their close liaison and consultation. The interchange of information with the author of the national anthems article in *The New Grove Dictionary of Music* has been most valuable.

The original idea for this book came from J. B. Cramer & Co. Ltd. who published a collection in the Second World War of National Anthems of the United Nations edited by Martin Shaw. Upon the death of Dr. Shaw in 1959, the musical editorship of National Anthems of the World was taken over by Dr. Henry Coleman. Upon Dr. Coleman's death in 1965, Dr. T. M. Cartledge, who had worked with him on the first and second editions, became musical editor, and is joined for this latest edition by Dr. W. L. Reed who has been responsible for most of the arrangements.

Acknowledgement is made at the foot of those anthems which are the copyright of J. B. Cramer & Co. Ltd. and other copyright material has been similarly acknowledged. Every effort has been made to trace copyright ownership, and it is regretted if any acknowledgements have been unwittingly omitted. In most cases the version in the melody and the accompaniment is that officially authorized by the State. Where piano arrangements and translations have been specially made, these may not be reproduced without the permission of Blandford Press Ltd.

Certain National Anthems have numerous verses, only one or two of which are customarily used, and so only these are given. Where English translations have been versified to fit the music, this has been done not so much for the purpose of singing (for the original language or languages would be used), but more to offer an indication of the meaning and so help in intelligent interpretation in singing the original words.

Where an anthem is in a language that is not written in the Latin alphabet, the words are given in a transliterated phonetic version to enable the anthem to be sung by those who cannot read it in its original form.

We must also acknowledge the help of many officials and individuals all over the world who have given much information on important details. They are too numerous to list individually. Mention must, however, be made of Mr. Michael Karl Blackshaw, who put at our disposal material which he had assembled for a book on the same subject. We acknowledge the advice of Mr. M. J. Bristow in the preparation of this fifth edition.

On various occasions we have consulted the Foreign Office, the Admiralty, the War Office, the BBC Music Library, the Royal Military School of Music, Kneller Hall, and the Royal Marines School of Music, and acknowledge their assistance.

The main reference books consulted are Paul Nettl's *National Anthems* (1952, Storm Publishers, New York), Grove's *Dictionary of Music* (Macmillan), Collier's Encyclopedia (1959, New York), Murillo's *National Anthem of Countries of North, Central and South America* (1935).

It is hoped that this fifth edition of National Anthems of the World will continue to be a useful source book, not only for the increasing number of occasions on which it is desired to sing or play a particular anthem, but also as a reference book of considerable interest (as it has already proved) and as a record of the aspirations of the whole family of nations.

AFGHANISTAN

Music transcribed and adapted from the band arrangement by T. M. CARTLEDGE

Transliterated version of Afghan words

SO CHE DA MEZAKA ASMAN WEE
SO CHE DA JAHAN WADAN WEE
SO CHE JOWAND PA DE JAHAN WEE
SO CHE PATI YAW AFGHAN WEE
TEL BA DA AFGHANISTAN WEE
TEL DE WEE AFGHANISTAN MELAT
TEL DE WEE JUMHOURIAT
TEL DE WEE MELI WAHDAT
TEL DE WEE AFGHAN MELI JUMHOURIAT
TEL DE WEE AFGHAN MELLAT JUMHOURIAT MELI WAHDAT
MELI WAHDAT

English Translation

So long as there is the earth and the heavens;
So long as the world endures;
So long as there is life in the world;
So long as a single Afghan breathes;
There will be this Afghanistan.

Long live the Afghan nation.
Long live the Republic.
Forever there be our national unity;
Forever there be the Afghan nation and the Republic.
Forever the Afghan nation, the Republic and National Unity –
National Unity.

ALBANIA

Hymni i Flamurit

Words by
ASDREN (A.S. DRENOVA)

Melody by
CIPRIAN PORUMBESCU (1880)
Arr. by HENRY COLEMAN

Alla marcia
f
Rreth flam - ur - it të për ba - shku - ar Me - një dë -
f

- shir e një që - llim; Të gjith at - je duk 'ju be -

pp
- tu - ar Të lid - him be - sën për shpë - tim. Prej
pp

Adopted as National Anthem, 1912

Free Translation

The flag which in battle unites us
Found us all ready for the oath,
One mind, one aim, until our land
Becomes free from the enemy.
We stand in the battle for right and freedom,
The enemies of the people stand alone,
The hero dedicates his life to our land,
Even in dying he will be brave.

ALGERIA

Qassaman

Words by
MUFDI ZAKARIA

Music by
MOHAMED FAWZI
Arr. by TAREK HASSAN

Tempo di Marcia
tr
Drum
ff
mp
1
2
Qa-ssa-man Bin-na-zi-la-t Il-ma-hi-qat Wad-di-
-maa Iz-za-ki-ya-t It-ta-hi-rat. Qa-ssa-
Ped.

Adopted as National Anthem in 1963

Mufdi Zakara, who wrote the words, is a celebrated contemporary Algerian poet; Mohamed Fawzi is an Egyptian musician.

2
Wal - bo - noo - d Il - la - mi - aa - t Il - kha - fi - qa - - t F'Il - gi
ff
bal Ish - sha - mi - kha - t Ish sha - hi - qa - - - t Nah - no Thur - na Fa ha -
-ya - ton Aw ma ma - at Wa A - qad - na Al - az - ma An Tah - ya Al - ga -
sf
- za - ir Fash - ha - doo Fash - ha - doo Fash - ha - doo.
sf
3
★

2. *Nah-no Gon-don Fi Sa-bi-l Il hakki Thor-na*
Wa I-la Iss-tiq-la-li-na Bil-har-bi Kum-na.
Lam Ya-kon Yoss-gha La-na Lam-ma Na-tak-na
Fat-ta-khath-na Ran-na-t Al-ba-roo-di Waz-na.
Wa Azaf-na Na-gha-ma-t Al-rash-sha-shi Lah-na
Wa A-qad-na Al-azma An Tah-ya Al-ga-za-ir.
Fash-ha-doo! Fash-ha-doo! Fash-ha-doo!

3. *Nah-no min Ab-ta-li-na Nad-fa-oo Gon-dan*
Wa A-la Ash-la-ina Nass-na-oo Mag-dan.
Wa A-la Ar-wa-he-na Nass-a-do Khul-dan
Wa A-la Ha-ma-ti-na Nar-fa-o Ban-dan.
Gab-ha-to'L-tah-ree-ri Aa-tay-na-ki Ah-dan
Wa A-qad-na Al-azma An Tah-ya Al-ga-za-ir.
Fash-ha-doo! Fash-ha-doo! Fash-ha-doo!

4. *Sar-kha-to'l-aw-ta-ni min Sa-h Il-fi-da*
Iss-ma-oo-ha Wass-ta-gee-bo Lin-ni-da
Wak-to-boo-ha Bi-di-maa Il-sho-ha-daa
Wak-ra-oo-ha Li-ba-ny Il-geeli gha-dan.
Kad Ma-dad-na La-ka Ya Mag-do Ya-da
Wa A-qad-na Al-azma An Tah-ya Al-ga-za-ir.
Fash-ha-doo! Fash-ha-doo! Fash-ha-doo!

French Translation

1. *Par les foudres qui anéantissent,*
Par les flots de sang pur et sans tache,
Par les drapeaux flottants qui flottent,
Sur les hauts djebels orgueilleux et fiers,
Nous jurons nous être révoltés pour vivre ou pour mourir,
Et nous avons juré de mourir pour que vive l'Algérie!*
Témoignez! Témoignez! Témoignez!

2. *Nous sommes des soldats pour la justice, révoltés,*
Et pour notre indépendance nous avons engagé le combat,
Nous n'avons obéi à nulle injonction en nous soulevant.
Le bruit de la poudre a été notre mesure
Et le crépitement des mitrailleuses notre chant favori.
Et nous avons juré de mourir pour que vive l'Algérie!
Témoignez! Témoignez! Témoignez!

3. *Sur nos héros nous bâtirons une gloire*
Et sur nos corps nous monterons à l'immortalité,
Sur nos âmes, nous construirons une armée
Et de notre espoir nous lèverons l'étendard.
Front de la libération, nous t'avons prêté serment
Et nous avons juré de mourir pour que vive l'Algérie!
Témoignez! Témoignez! Témoignez!

4. *Le cri de la patrie monte des champs de bataille.*
Ecoutez-le et répondez à l'appel.
Ecrivez-le dans le sang des martyrs
Et dictez-le aux générations futures.
Nous t'avons donné la main, ô gloire,
Et nous avons juré de mourir pour que vive l'Algérie!
Témoignez! Témoignez! Témoignez!

* litt. "SERMENT" peut se traduire par "Nous jurons" ou "nous avons juré".

English Translation by T. M. Cartledge.
(from the French)

1. We swear by the lightning that destroys,
By the streams of generous blood being shed,
By the bright flags that wave,
Flying proudly on the high djebels,
That we are in revolt, whether to live or to die,
We are determined that Algeria should live,
So be our witness- be our witness- be our witness.

2. We are soldiers in revolt for truth
And through war we try to get our Independence.
When we spoke, nobody listened to us,
So we have taken the noise of gunpowder as our rhythm
And the sound of machine-guns as our melody,
We are determined that Algeria should live,
So be our witness- be our witness- be our witness.

3. From our heroes we shall make an army come to being,
From our dead we shall build up a glory,
Our spirits shall ascend to immortality
And on our shoulders we shall raise the Standard.
To the nation's Liberation Front we have sworn an oath
We are determined that Algeria should live,
So be our witness- be our witness- be our witness.

4. The cry of the Fatherland sounds. from the battle-fields.
Listen to it and answer the call!
Let it be written with the blood of martyrs
And be read to future generations.
Oh, Glory, we have held out our hand to you
We are determined that Algeria should live,
So be our witness- be our witness- be our witness.

ANDORRA

Words by
The Hon. Dr. D. JOAN BENLLOCH I VIVÓ
(1864-1926)

Music by
Father ENRIC MARFANY
(1871-1942)

Energico
f
El gran Car - le-many, mon Pa - - - - re, dels a-
-larbs me des - lliu - rá, i del cel vi - daem do-
-ná de Me - rit - xell la gran Ma - re. Prin -

This became officially the National Anthem on the 8th September 1914,
the anniversary day of the Jungfrau von Meritxell, patron saint of Andorra.

- ce - sa nasquí i Pu - bi - lla en - tre dos na - cions neu -
- tral; Sols res - to l'ú - ni - ca fi - lla del im-
- pe - - ri Car - le - many. Cre - ient i lliu - re on - se
se - gles, cre - ient i lliu - re vull ser.

ff
rall.
fff
¡Si - guen els furs mos tu - tors i mos Prín-ceps de - fen - sors! i mos
ff rall. con canto
fff
rall. più
a tempo
Prín - ceps de - fen - sors!
rall. più
mf a tempo
cresc.
p
cresc.

Free Translation

The great Charlemagne, my Father, from the Saracens liberated me, and from heaven he gave me life of Meritxell the great Mother. I was born a Princess, a Maiden neutral between two nations; I am the only remaining daughter of the Carolingian empire. Believing and free eleven centuries, believing and free I will be. The laws of the land be my tutors and my defender Princes! and my defender Princes!

ARGENTINE

Words by
VICENTE LÓPEZ Y PLANES
(1784-1856)
Music by
BLAS PARERA (b. 1777)
Arr. by
JUAN PEDRO ESNAOLA (1808-1878)
Maestoso
VERSE
¡O-id; mor-
-ta - les! el gri - to sa - gra - do; ¡Li - ber-
-tad, li - ber-tad, li - ber - tad! O-id el

Officially adopted as National Anthem, 11th May 1813, by the General Constituent Assembly of Argentina

rui - do de ro - tas ca - de - nas; Ved en
tro - na a la no - ble I-gual-dad.
ff
p
¡Ya su tro - no dig-ní - si - mo a - brie - ron Las Pro -
p
f
f
- vin - cias U - ni - das del Sud! Y los
p

li - bres del mun - do res - pon - den: ¡Al gran
p
pue - blo Ar - gen - ti - no, Sa - lud! ¡Al gran
mf
mf
pue - blo Ar - gen - ti - no, Sa - lud! Y los
li - bres del mun - do res - pon - den ¡Al gran
p
f
p

mf
pue - blo Ar - gen - ti - no, Sa - lud! Y los
mf
li - bres del mun - do res - pon - den ¡Al gran
f
mf
pue - blo Ar - gen - ti - no, Sa - lud!
f

CHORUS
Allegro vivace
Sean e - ter - nos los lau - re - les. Que su - pi - mos con - se -
- guir: Que su - pi - mos con - se - guir: Co - ro -
Lento
lunga
Allegro vivace
- na - dos de glo - ria vi - va - - - mos O ju -
- re - mos con glo - ria mo - rir. O ju -

Free Translation

Hear, oh mortals! the sacred cry:
Freedom, freedom, freedom!
Hear the noise of broken chains;
See the throne of Equality the noble.

The United Provinces of the South
Their throne full of dignity opened!
And the free of the world reply:
A salutation to the great Argentine people!

CHORUS Let those laurels be eternal
Which we knew how to win:
Let us live crowned by glory
Or swear with glory to die.

AUSTRALIA

Advance Australia Fair

Music by
PETER DODDS McCORMICK
("AMICUS") (1835-1916)
Arr. by H. A. CHAMBERS

Maestoso
f
Aus - tra - lia's sons, let us re-joice, For we are young and free; We've
f

mf
gold - en soil and wealth for toil, Our home is girt by sea. Our
mf

Written in 1878, this has been used for some years as a national song.
The national anthem is "God Save the Queen".

land a-bounds in Na - ture's gifts Of beau - ty rich and rare; In
his - t'ry's page let ev - 'ry stage Ad - vance Aus - tra - lia fair.
f
f
CHORUS (S.A.T.B.)
mf
cresc.
ff
In joy - ful strains then let us sing, "Ad - vance Aus - tra - lia fair."
ff
mf
cresc.
mf
cresc.
ff

AUSTRIA

Officially adopted as National Anthem by Austrian Cabinet 25th February 1947

*Later research shows it is doubtful that Mozart was the composer.
The melody was added to masonic cantata K.623 published after his death.

Volk, be - gna - det für das Schö - ne, Viel - ge - rühm - tes
ho - her Sen - dung Last ge - tra - gen, Viel - ge - prüf - tes
Ö - ster - reich. Viel - ge - rühm - tes Ö - ster - reich.
Ö - ster - reich. Viel - ge - prüf - tes Ö - ster - reich.

3. *Mutig in die neuen Zeiten,*
frei und gläubig sieh uns schreiten,
arbeitsfroh und hoffnungsreich.
Einig laß in Brüderchören,
Vaterland, dir Treue schwören,
Vielgeliebtes Österreich. (bis)

Free Translation

1. Land of mountains, land of streams, land of fields, land of spires, land of hammers, with a rich future, you are the home of great sons, a nation blessed by its sense of beauty,
highly praised Austria, highly praised Austria.

2. Strongly fought for, fiercely contested, you are in the centre of the Continent like a strong heart, you have borne since the earliest days the burden of a high mission,
much tried Austria, much tried Austria.

3. Watch us striding free and believing, with courage, into new eras, working cheerfully and full of hope, in fraternal chorus let us take in unity the oath of allegiance to you, our country,
our much beloved Austria, our much beloved Austria.

BAHAMAS

March on, Bahamaland!

* Words and Music by
TIMOTHY GIBSON (1969)
Arr. by W. L. REED

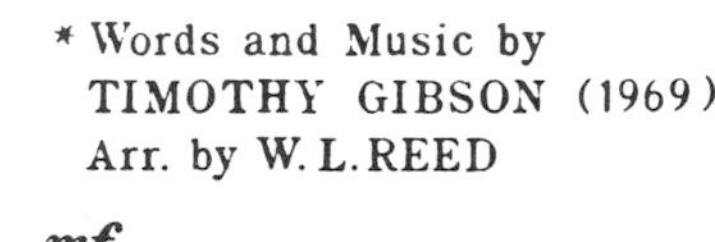

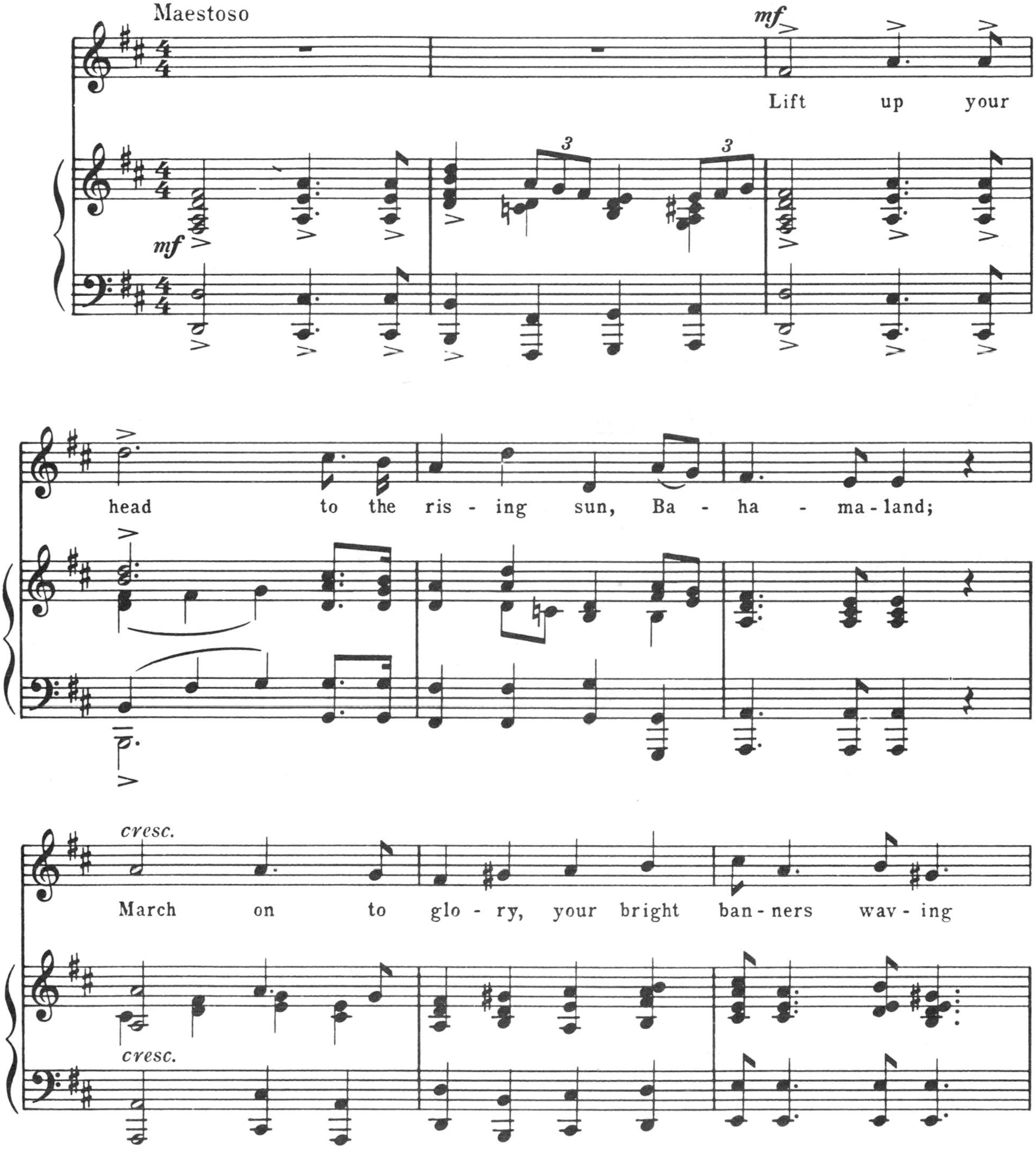

Maestoso
mf
Lift up your
mf
head to the ris - ing sun, Ba - ha - ma - land;
cresc.
March on to glo - ry, your bright ban - ners wav - ing
cresc.

Selected as a result of a competition and adopted when the Bahamas became independent in 1973.

mf
high. See how the world marks the
mf
man - ner of your bear - ing! Pledge to ex - cel through
mp
cresc.
love and_ un - i - ty. Press-ing on - ward, march to-
mp
cresc.
-ge - ther to a com - mon loft - ier goal; Stead - y

poco rit.
sun - ward, though the wea - ther hide the wide and treach - 'rous
poco rit.
allargando
f Grandioso
shoal. Lift up your head to the
allargando
f
ff
ris - ing sun, Ba - ha - ma - land; 'Til the road you've trod Lead un-
ff
- to your God, March on, Ba - ha - ma - land!

BAHRAIN

No words

BANGLADESH

Words and Music by
RABINDRANATH TAGORE (1861-1941)

Music supervised by
SAMAR DAS
Arranged by
T. M. CARTLEDGE

Ā - mār so - nār Bām - lā, Ā - mi to - māý
bhā - lo - bā - si, Ci - rā - din to - mār
ā - kās, to - mār bā - tas, ā - mār prā - né
O - mā ā - mār prā - né bā - jāý bā - śi. So - nār

Officially adopted in April 1971 by the then provisional government; approved by the National Assembly of Bangladesh on 13 January 1972

Bām - lā, Ā - mi to - māý bhā - lo -
- bā - si. O - mā, Fā - gu - ne tor
kū - le mā, tor mu-kher bā - nī
ā - mer ba - ne ghrā - ne pā - gal' ka - re,
ā - mār kā - ne lā - ge, su - dhar ma - to,
ma - ri hāý, hāý re - o - mā,
ma - ri hāý, hāý re - mā, tor

2nd time
to
Fā-gu - ne tor__ ā - mer__ ba - ne__ ghrā - ne____ pā - gal ka - re,___
mu-kher bā - nī__ ā - mar__ ka - ne__ lā - ge,____ su-dhar mo - to,___
O - mā a - ghrā - ne tor__ bha - rā
— mā, tor ba - dan - khā - ni__ ma - lin
kse - te__ kī__ de - khe - chi____ ā - mi kī de -
ha - le,__ ā - mi__ na - ýan____ O - mā ā - mi
- khe - chi__ ma-dhur hā - si__ So - nār__ Bām - lā___
nā - ýān - ja - lé bhā - si,__ So - nār__ Bām - lā___

Fine
ā - mi to - māẏ bhā - lo bā - si,
ā - mi to - māẏ bhā - lo bā - si.
Fine
kī so - bhā, kī chā - ẏā go kī
sne - ha, kī mā - ẏā go kī ā - cal bi - chā -
- ye - chā - ba - ter mū - le, na - dīr kū - le
D. 𝄋 al fine

English Translation

Oh, my Golden Bengal
  I love thee.
Oh, mother mine
  thy skies, thy air always
Make my heart sing.

Oh, mother mine
  in the month of Falgun,
in thy mango-groves
The fragrance makes me ecstatic.

Oh, mother mine
  in the month of Aghrayan
what beauty do I behold
in thy fields full of corn;
what beauty, what shades, what love,
What tenderness, oh!

Oh, mother mine
  thou spreadest thy wonderful skirt
under the banyan tree,
On the banks of the river.

Oh, mother mine
  thy words seem to my ears like nectar;
Oh, what rapture, what ecstasy!

Oh, mother mine
  if thy face falls
Tears stream down my cheeks.

BARBADOS

This anthem was adopted on 30th November, 1966, when Barbados attained Independence.

stood, That binds our hearts from coast to coast- The
free, And great - er will our na - tion grow In
pride of na - tion - hood.
strength and u - ni - ty.
CHORUS
ff
We loy - al sons and
ff
daugh - ters all Do here - by make it known These
fields and hills be - yond re - call Are now our ve - ry

mf
own. We write our names on his - tory's page With
mf
f
ex - pec - ta - tions great, Strict guard - ians of our
f
cresc. rall. ff
he - ri - tage, Firm crafts - men of our fate.
cresc. rall. ff

BELGIUM

La Brabançonne

Words by
CHARLES ROGIER (1800-1885)
English translation of the French words by
MARY ELIZABETH SHAW and DICCON SHAW

Music by
FRANÇOIS VAN CAMPENHOUT (1779-1848)

Fieramente, non allegro
f
A-près des siè - cles d'es - cla - va - ge, Le
O dier-baar Bel - gië, o heil - ig land der vaa - dren, on - ze
From out the tomb of bond - age and sla - ve - ry Has
f
Bel - ge, sor-tant du tom - beau, A re - con-
ziel en ons hart zijn U ge - wijd. Aan-vaard ons
Bel - gium at last ris - en free; And has re-
-quis par son cou - ra - ge Son
kracht en het bloed van ons aa - dren, wees ons
-cov - ered by her bra - ve - ry, Her

Written and composed during the 1830 revolution. The original French words were by Jenneval, a Belgian officer, but the present version was written in 1860 by Prime Minister Charles Rogier. The Dutch text also underwent several changes. The present version was officially adopted in 1938 – it is a different text from the French.

mf
nom, ses droits et son dra - peau. Et ta
doel in ar - beid en in strijd. Bloei, o
name, her flag, her lib - er - ty; And by your
mf
main sou - ve - raine et fiè - re, Peu -
land, in een - dracht niet te bre - ken, Wees
mien undaunt - ed and vic - tor - ious Since that
più f
-ple dé - sor - mais in - domp - té, Gra -
im - mer U zelf en on - ge - knecht Het woord ge -
day, up - hold - ing your cause, Is bla - zoned
più f

-va sur ta vieil - le ban - niè - re: Le
-trouw dat ge on - be-vreesd moogt spre - ken, Voor
on your an - cient ban - ner glor - ious, Your
Roi, La Loi, La Li - ber - té, Gra -
Vorst, voor vrij - heid en voor recht, Het woord ge -
King, your free - dom and your laws, Is bla - zoned
-va sur ta vieil - le ban - niè - re: Le
trouw dat ge on - be-vreesd moogt spre - ken, Voor
on your an - cient ban - ner glor - ious, Your
f
f

ff
Roi, La Loi, La Li - ber - té, Le
Vorst, voor vrij - heid en voor recht, Voor
King, your free - dom and your laws, Your
ff
poco allarg.
Roi, La Loi, La Li - ber - té, Le
Vorst, voor vrij - heid en voor recht, Voor
King, your free - dom and your laws, Your
poco allarg.
Roi, La Loi, La Li - ber - té.
Vorst, voor vrij - heid en voor recht.
King, your free - dom and your laws.

BELIZE

Land of the Gods

Words by
SAMUEL A. HAYNES

Music by
S. WALFORD YOUNG
Arranged from orchestral version by
W. L. REED

Maestoso
1. O land of the Gods by the Ca - rib Sea, Our
2. Na - ture has blessed thee with wealth un - told, O'er
man - hood we pledge to thy li - ber - ty. No
moun - tains and val - leys where prai - ries roll. Our
ty - rants here lin - ger, des - pots must flee This
fa - thers the Bay - men, va - liant and bold, Drove

p
tran - quil ha - ven of de - mo - cra - cy. The
back th'in - va - der, this he - ri - tage hold. From
p
blood of our sires which hal - lows the sod Brought
proud Ri - o Hon - do to Old Sar - stoon, Through
cresc.
f
free - dom from slav - 'ry, op - pres - sion's rod. By the
co - ral isle, o - ver blue la - goon, Keep
cresc.
f
might of truth and the grace of God No
watch with the an - gels, the stars and moon, For

lon - ger shall we be hew - ers of wood.
free - dom comes to - mor - row's noon.
CHORUS
ff
A - rise ye sons of the
ff
Bay - men's clan! Put on your
ar - mour, clear the land! Drive

back the ty - rants, let
des - pots flee!
allargando
Land of the Gods by the Ca -
allargando
rib Sea.

BENIN PEOPLE'S REPUBLIC

L'Aube Nouvelle

THE DAWN OF A NEW DAY

Words and music by the Abbé G. DAGNON
Arr. by HENRY COLEMAN

Adopted as the National Anthem at the declaration of independence, August, 1960
The chorus is usually sung on its own.

-vrer au prix du sang des com - bats é - cla - tants. Ac-cou-
-rez vous aus-si, bâ - tis - seurs du pré - sent, Plus forts dans
l'u - ni - té, chaqu' jour à la tâ - che, Pour la
pos - té - ri - té, cons - trui - sez sans re - lâ - che.

CHORUS
ff
En - fants du Bé – nin, de - bout! La
ff
li - ber - té d'un cri so - no - re Chante aux pre-miers feux de l'au-
- ro - re; En-fants du Bé – nin, de - bout!

2. *Quand partout souffle un vent de colère et de haine,*
Béninois, sois fier, et d'une âme sereine,
Confiant dans l'avenir, regarde ton drapeau!
Dans le vert tu liras l'espoir du renouveau,
De tes aïeux le rouge èvoque le courage;
Des plus riches trésors le jaune est le présage.

3. Tes monts ensoleillés, tes palmiers, ta verdure,
Cher Bénin, partout font ta vive parure.
Ton sol offré à chacun la richesse des fruits.
Bénin, désormais que tes fils tous unis
D'un fraternel élan partagent l'espérance
De te voir à jamais heureux dans l'abondance.

English Paraphrase by
ELIZABETH P. COLEMAN

Chorus

Children of Bénin, arise!
The resounding cry of freedom
Is heard at the first light of dawn;
Children of Bénin, arise!

1. Formerly, at her call, our ancestors
Knew how to engage in mighty battles
With strength, courage, ardour, and full of joy, but at the price of blood.
Builders of the present, you too, join forces
Each day for the task stronger in unity
Build without ceasing for posterity.

2. When all around there blows a wind of anger and hate:
Citizen of Bénin be proud, and in a calm spirit
Trusting in the future, behold your flag!
In the green you read hope of spring;
The red signifies the courage of your ancestors;
The yellow foretells the richest treasures.

3. Beloved Bénin, your sunny mountains, palm trees, and green pastures
Show everywhere your brightness;
Your soil offers everyone the richest fruits.
Bénin, from henceforth your sons are united
With one brotherly spirit sharing the hope of seeing you
Enjoy abundance and happiness for ever.

BHUTAN

Royal Anthem

Transcribed and arranged by
W. L. REED

BOLIVIA

Words by
JOSE IGNACIO de SANJINÉS
(1786-1864)
Translated by
G. H. HATCHMAN
Versified by
SEBASTIAN SHAW

Music by
BENEDETTO VINCENTI

Played for first time in 1842 and adopted the same year.
José de Sanjinés was a jurist and signer of the Bolivian Declaration of Independence.

li - bre ya li - bre es - te sue - - lo, ya ce -
free - dom, our free - dom, is found now, E - ver from
- só su ser-vil con - di - ción. Al es -
bon - dage we cel - e - brate re - lease. Af - ter
mf
f
- truen - do marcial que a - yer fue - - ra y al cla -
all the mar - tial clam - our that as - pires To the
- mor de la gue - rra ho - rro - ro - - so, si - guen
clash of war - fare's hi - de-ous in - sa - ni - ty, Now in

hoy en con-tras - te ar - mo - nio - - - so dul - ces
con - trast hear the mu - sic of hu - ma - ni - ty, Joy - ful
him - nos de paz y de u - nión. Si - guen
hymns of sweet u - ni - ty and peace. Now in
cresc.
hoy en con-tras - te ar - mo - nio - - - so dul - ces
con - trast hear the mu - sic of hu - ma - ni - ty, Joy - ful
cresc.
him - nos de paz y de u - nión. De la
hymns of sweet u - ni - ty and peace. E - ver -
f CHORUS
ff
f

Pa - - - tria, el al - to nom - - - - bre en glo -
- more, Moth - er-land, the na - - - - tion Shall pre -
- rio - so es - plen - dor con - ser - ve - - - - mos y en sus
- serve your glor - ious name's fair re - pu - ta - - - - tion. Hear, oh
a - ras de nuevo ju - re - - - mos, ¡Mo - rir an - tes que es-cla - vos vi -
al - tars, our de-di - ca - - - tion Rath - er death than ex-is - tence as
- vir! ¡Mo - rir an - tes que es-cla - vos vi - vir! ¡Mo - rir
slaves, Rath - er death than ex-is - tence as slaves, Rath - er
ff

2. *Esta tierra inocente y hermosa*
que ha debido a Bolívar su nombre,
es la Patria feliz donde el hombre
goza el bien de la dicha y la paz.
Que los hijos del grande Bolívar
han ya mil y mil veces jurado
morir antes que ver humillado
de la Patria el augusto pendón.

CORO: De la Patria etc.

3. *Loor eterno a los bravos guerreros*
cuyo heróico valor y firmeza
conquistaron las glorias que empieza
hoy Bolivia feliz a gozar.
Que sus nombres el mármol y el bronce
a remotas edades trasmitan
y en sonoros cantares repitan
¡Libertad, Libertad, Libertad!

CORO: De la Patria etc.

2. Here where Justice has raised up her throne,
Long denied her by the evil of oppression,
Her flung banners find glorious expression
We are free, we are free, we are free!
Sons, whom mighty Bolivar shall call his own,
Have a thousand thousand times in great solemnity
Freely offered life itself as sworn indemnity,
If dishonoured their flag should ever be.

CHORUS: Evermore, Motherland etc.

3. Those brave warriors eternally praise,
Whose courage, unexampled, evermore is
The foundation of all the proud glories
To which happy Bolivia is heir.
Lettered bronze and marble gratefully we'll raise
That their deeds may live for distant generations,
And our sons' and grandsons' joyful salutations
Shall, in song, honour still the great names there.

CHORUS: Evermore, Motherland etc.

BOTSWANA
(Fatshe la rona)

Officially adopted 30 September 1966, when Botswana became independent.

BRAZIL

Words by
JOAQUIM OSÓRIO DUQUE ESTRADA
(1870-1927)
Translated by
GASTAO NOTHMAN
Versified by
SEBASTIAN SHAW

Music by
FRANCESCO MANUEL da SILVA
(1795-1865)

The music was written for the National Anthem in 1831 on the accession of Emperor D. Pedro II. In 1922 a new text was officially adopted and the same tune retained.

VERSE
1. Ou - vi - ram do Y - pi-ran - ga as mar - gens
1. From peace - ful Y - pi-ran - ga's banks rang
plá - ci - das De um po - vo he-roi - co o bra - do re - tum -
out a cry, A chal - lenge from a peo - ple who were
- ban - te, E o sol da li - ber-da - de em rá - ios
fear - less; Thence - forth the sun of Free - dom climbed our
fúl - gi - dos, Bri - lhou no céu da Pá - tria nes - se in
coun - try's sky, And poured its rays up - on us, bright and

stan - te, Se o pe - nhor des-sa i - gual - da - de Con - se -
peer - less. We, with breasts bared, de - fy, oh Free - dom, Death it -
- gui - mos con - quis - tar com bra - ço for - te, Em teu
- self, for the e - qua - li - ty you taught us! Striv - ing
sei - o, Oh, Li - ber - da - de, De - sa -
fierce - ly, here in your bo - som, To be
- fi - a o nos - so pei - to a prò - pria mor - te! Oh! Pá - tria a -
worth - y of this prec - ious gift you brought us. O glor - ious

pp
- ma - da‿i - do - la - tra - da, Sal - ve! Sal - ve! Bra -
and be - lov - ed land, hail! Hail Bra - zil! Be -
pp
cresc.
- sil, um so - nho‿in-ten - so‿um rá - io vi - vi - do De‿a -
- hold a won - drous vi - sion, lo! a dazz - ling ray Of
cresc.
cresc.
- mor e de‿es - pe - ran - ça‿à ter - ra des - ce, Se‿em
love and hope, from heav'n to earth, trans - cen - dent! Our
cresc.
teu for - mo - so céu, ri - so - nho‿e lím - pi - do, A‿i -
smil - ing skies, in lim - pid beau - ty, now dis - play A

p
- ma - gem do cru - zei - ro res - plan - de - ce. Gi -
war - rior's form, gi - gan - tic and res - plen - dent. Whence
p
- gan - te pe - la pró - pria na - tu - re - - za, Es
spring such beau - ty, brave - ry and strength so rare? Oh!
be - lo‿és for - te‿im - pá - vi - do co - los - so. E‿o
might - y vis - ion, well we know that we sur - vey Our
CHORUS
ff
teu fu - tu - ro‿es - pe - lha‿es - sa gran - de - za. Ter - ra‿a - do -
coun - try's fu - ture great - ness shown for us there. A - mongst a
ff

-ra - da, en-tre ou-tras mil, és tu, Bra - sil, Oh! Pá-tria a -
thou - sand, You ev - er will Be, oh Bra - zil, The one dear
-ma - da! dos fi - lhos des - te so - lo és mãe gen -
home - land! Oh bount-eous mo - ther, with such love you
-til, Pá - tria a-ma - da, Bra - sil!
fill Your proud chil - dren, Bra - zil!
1
tr
f
tr
2
-sil!
-zil!
f cresc.
ff

2. *Deitado eternamente em berço esplêndido,*
Ao som do mar e à luz do ceu profundo,
Fulguras, Brasil, florão da América,
Iluminado ao sol do novo mundo.
Do que a terra mais garrida
Teus risonhos, lindos campos têm mais flores,
Nossos bosques têm mais vida,
Nossa vida no teu seio mais amores.
Oh! Pátria amada, idolatrada,
Salve! Salve!
Brasil, de amor eterno seja o símbolo
O lábaro que ostentas estrelado,
E diga o verde louro dessa flâmula
Paz no futuro e glória no passado.
Mas, se ergues da justiça a clava forte
Verás que um filho teu não foge à luta
Nem teme quem te adora a própria morte.
Terra adorada entre, outras mil, és tu, Brasil,
Oh! Pátria amada! dos filhos deste solo és mãe gentil,
Pátria amada, Brasil!

2. To ocean's music, under skies of deepest blue,
America's fair flower, fading never,
In splendour you lie cradled. Oh Brazil, on you
The sun of this New World shines down for ever!
Oh, far more than in fair lands elsewhere,
Your sweet pastures are bedecked with smiling blossom;
Your vast woodlands a greater life share,
And a deeper love we know within your bosom.
Oh glorious and beloved land, hail! Hail Brazil!
Then let your starry ensign never cease to fly,
Symbolic of the love that fills your story;
And let the verdant laurels on your pennon cry:-
"In future peace and in the past great glory!"
But if, in justice, you should raise your mighty sword,
You shall not see a son of yours from battle flee,
Nor shall he fear to die for you, whom he adored.
Amongst a thousand,
You ever will
Be, oh Brazil,
The one dear homeland!
Oh bounteous mother, with such love you fill
Your proud children, Brazil!

BRUNEI

Words by
PENGIRAN MAHOMED YUSUF bin
PENGIRAN HAJI ABDUL RAHIM (b. 1923)

Music by
INCHE AWANG BESAR bin SAGAP (b. 1914)
Arr. by HENRY COLEMAN

Moderato
ff
Ya Al - lah lan - jut - kan lah u - si - a
ff
Du - li tu - an - ku yang ma - ha mu - li - a
A - dil ber - dau - lat me - naung - i no - sa

This anthem was composed in 1947 through the initiative of a group of youths who decided that their country should have a National Anthem, and chose two of their number to write and compose it. It was officially adopted in 1951.

Free Translation

Oh God, Long Live our Majesty the Sultan;
Justice and Sovereignty in sheltering our country and leading our people;
Prosperity to our Nation and Sultan.
God Save Brunei.

BULGARIA

Shoumi Maritsa

Words by
MARAČEK
Revised by NIKOLO SCHIWKOW (1847-1901)

Music by
GABRIEL SEBEK
Arr. by HENRY COLEMAN

Marziale
p
1. Shou - mi Ma - ri - tsa o - kar-va - ve - na,
p

mf
Pla - che vdo - vi - tsa, lyu - to ra - ne - na.
mf

f
Marsh, marsh, s'ge - ne - ra - la na - sh,
f

This National Anthem dates from the year 1885, but is not at present sung inside Bulgaria.

2. *Balgarsky cheda, tsyal svyat vi gleda,*
V' boy za pobeda, slavno da varvim.
Marsh, marsh s'Generala nash,
v'boy da letim i vrag da pobedim!

3. *Lavat Balkansky, v'boy velikansky,*
s'ordi doushmansky, vodi ni krilat.
Marsh, marsh s' Generala nash,
v'boy da letim i vrag da pobedim!

English Translation

1. Maritsa rushes, stained with blood,
A widow wails, fiercely wounded.
March, march, with our General,
Let's fly into battle and crush the enemy!

2. Bulgarians, the whole world beholds you.
Into a winning battle, let's gloriously go.
March, march, with our General,
Let's fly into battle and crush the enemy!

3. The Balkan lion leads us flying
Into a gigantic battle with the enemy hordes.
March, march, with our General,
Let's fly into battle and crush the enemy!

BULGARIA

Words by TSVETAN TSVETKOV RADOSLAVOV (1863-1931) (Verse 1 and Refrain)
PAVEL MATEV and GEORGI DJAGAROV (Verses 2 & 3)

Music by TSVETAN TSVETKOV RADOSLAVOV
Arr. by PANCHO VLADIGEROV, PARASHKEV HADJIEV, ALEXANDER RAICHEV

Andante maestoso (♩ = 66)

VERSE

mf ff mf

1. Gor - da Sta - ra
2. Pad - na - ha bor -
3. Droozh - no, brat - ya

pla - nee - na, do ne-yee Doo - na - va see - ne-yee, slun - tse Tra - kee-ya
- tsee bez-chet za na - ro - da nash lyu-bim. Ma-yee - ko, da-yee nee
Bul - ga - ree, s nas Mos - kva e v meer i v bo-yee! Par - tee - ya ve -

Trpts.

f

o - grya - va nad Pe - ree - na pla - men - e-yee.
muzh - ka see - la put - ya eem da pro - dul - zheem!
- lee - ka vo - dee nash - ee - ya po - bye - den stro-yee!

f

Original words and music were composed by Radoslavov while still a student in 1885, and on his way to fight in the Serbo - Bulgarian War. It quickly became popular. It was arranged as the National Anthem, replacing the previous Republican Anthem in 1964.

Notes: ◡ = blended into diphthong
Zh = as S in PLEASURE
U = very short, as O in MONEY
H = as CH in Scottish LOCH

CHORUS
Mee - la Ro-dee - no, (Ro-dee-no), tee see ze-men ra-yee,
tvo-yee - ta hu-bost, tvo-yee - ta pre-lest, ah, te nya - mat
1
kray-ee!
2
kray-ee!
Last time
kray-ee!

1. Proudly rise the Balkan peaks,
   At their feet Blue Danube flows;
   Over Thrace the sun is shining,
   Pirin looms in purple glow.

   REFRAIN
   Oh, dear native land,
   Earthly paradise!
   For your loveliness, your beauty
   E'er will charm our eyes.

2. Countless warriors bravely fell
   For the people's sacred cause;
   Give us strength and firmness, Mother,
   Guide us on the road they chose.
   REFRAIN

3. Be as one, Bulgarians!
   Moscow stands by us again;
   For our valiant Party leads us
   On to victory and fame!
   REFRAIN

Translated by Katya Boyadjieva

BURMA

This officially became the National Anthem in **1948**.

* The notes between asterisks may be sung an octave higher.

★ At the end of the anthem it is customary for the singers to give a slight bow.

BURUNDI

Uburundi Bwacu

French translation by
JEAN BATISTE NTAHOKAJA

Music by a commission presided over by l'Abbé
JEAN BATISTE NTAHOKAJA
Music prepared by l'Abbé
MARC BARENGAYABO
Arr. by W. L. REED

Adopted June 1962

Burundi bwacu, Burundi buhire
Shinga icumu mu mashinga
Gaba intahe y'ubugabo ku bugingo
Warapfunywe ntiwapfuye,
Warahubishijwe ntiwahababuka
Uhagurukana, uhagurukana, uhagurukana ubugabo urikukira
Komerwa amashyi n'amakungu
Habwa impundu n'abawe
Isamirane mu mashinga, isamirane mu mashinga,
Burundi bwacu, ragi ry'abasokuru
Ramutswa intahe n'ibuhugu
Ufatanije ishyaka n'ubuhizi
Vuza impundu wiganzuye uwakuganza
Burundi bwacu, nkora-mutima kuri twese
Tugutuye amoboko, umutima n'ubuzima
Imana yakuduhaye ikudutungire
Horana ubumwe n'abagabo n'itekane
Sagwa n'urweze, sagwa n'amahoro meza.

French Translation by Jean Batiste Ntahokaja

Cher Burundi, ô doux pays,
Prends place dans le concert des nations.
En tout bien, tout honneur, accéde á l'independance.
Mutilé et meurtri, tu es demeuré maître de toi-même.
L'heure venue, tu t'es levé
Et fièrement tu t'es hissè au rang des peuples libres.
Reçois donc le compliment des nations,
Agrée l'hommage de tes enfants.
Qu'à travers l'univers retentisse ton nom.
Cher Burundi, héritage sacré de nos aïeux,
Reconnu digne de te gouverner,
Au courage tu allies le sentiment de l'honneur.
Chante la gloire de ta liberté reconquise.
Cher Burundi, digne objet de notre plus tendre amour,
A ton noble service nous vouons nos bras, nos coeurs et nos vies.
Veuille Dieu, qui nous a fait don de toi, te conserver à notre vénération,
Sous l'égide de l'Unité,
Dans la paix, la joie et la prospérité.

English Translation (of French Version)
by T. M. Cartledge

Beloved Burundi, gentle country,
Take your place in the concert of nations,
Acceding to independence with honourable intentions.
Wounded and bruised, you have remained master of yourself.

When the hour came, you arose,
Lifting yourself proudly into the ranks of free peoples.
Receive, then, the congratulations of the nations
And the homage of your sons.
May your name ring out through the universe.

Beloved Burundi, sacred heritage from our forefathers,
Recognised as worthy of self-government,
With your courage you also have a sense of honour.
Sing the glory of liberty conquered again.

Beloved Burundi, worthy of our tenderest love,
We vow to your noble service our hands and hearts and lives.
May God, who gave you to us, keep you for us to venerate,
Under the shield of unity.
In peace, joy and prosperity.

CAMEROON

Chant de Ralliement

Words by RENÉ JAM AFAME
and a group of students
English versification by
T. M. CARTLEDGE

Music by
SAMUEL MINKYO BAMBA
and MOISE. NYATE
Arr. by HENRY COLEMAN

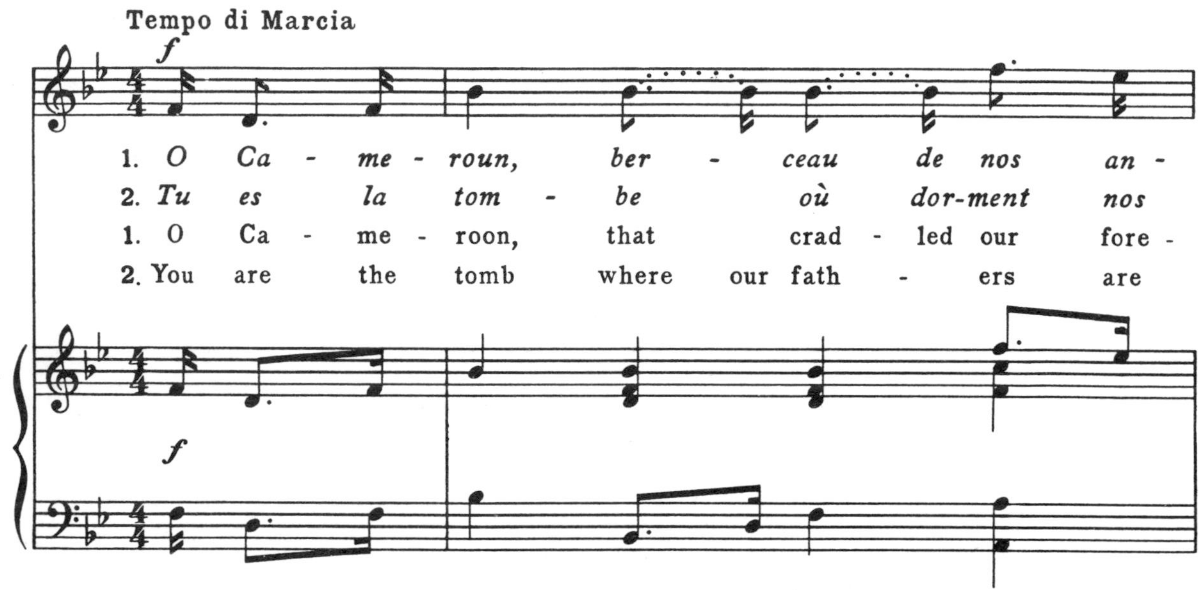

This anthem was written and composed in 1928 by students from l'Ecole Normale de la Mission Presbytérienne Américaine de Foulassi à Sangmelina, Cameroun. It was adopted as the unofficial National Anthem in 1948 and became the official Anthem on 10th May, 1957

- rie. Comme un so - leil tu commences à pa -
- vé. Nous tra - vail - lons pour te ren - dre pros -
days. But like the ris - ing sun now ap -
- ceived. We work that you may be-come fair and
- raî - tre; Peu à peu tu sors de ta sau-va - ge -
- pè - re, Un beau jour en-fin nous se - rons ar - ri -
- pear - ing, Bit by bit you now are leav - ing sav - age
pros - p'rous, And one day at last we'll see it all a -
- ri - e. Que tous tes en-fants du Nord au Sud, De
- vés. De l'A - fri - que soit fi - dèle en - fant Et
ways. May all your child-ren fol - low the com-mand, From
- chieved. May you be a faith-ful child of Af - ri - ca, Advancing

l'Est à l'Ouest soient tout a - mour. Te ser - vir que ce soit leur seul
pro-gres-se tou - jours en Paix, Es-pé-rant que tes jeunes en -
East and West to give their heart, Their on - ly wish to serve their
stead-i - ly in peace, In hope that ev - 'ry young child of
but Et rem - plir leur de - voir tou-jours.
-fants T'ai - me - ront sans bornes à ja - mais.
land And with con - stan - cy all play their part.
yours Will love you un - til time shall cease.
CHORUS
ff
Chère Pa - tri - - - e, terre ché - ri - - - e, Tu
This our land that we all love so, On
ff

es no - tre seul et vrai bon - heur. No - tre
you our whole hap - pi - ness is stayed. You're our
Ped. *
joi - e, no - tre vi - e, A toi l'a -
joy and you're our life too; To you be
Ped. *
3
- mour et le grand hon - neur!
hon - our and love dis - played.
Ped. *

CANADA

O CANADA

Words by
Sir Adolphe Basile Routhier (1839-1920)
English version by
R. STANLEY WEIR (1856-1926)

Music by
C. LAVALLÉE (1842-1891)
Arr. by H. A. CHAMBERS

The main anthem is that of Great Britain.

mf
fleu - rons glo - ri - eux! Car ton bras sait por - ter l'é -
dit en es - pé - rant. Il est né d'u - ne ra - ce
all thy sons com - mand. With glow - ing hearts we
lord - ly riv - ers flow, How dear to us thy
mf
- pé - e, Il sait por - ter la croix! Ton his -
fiè - re, Bé - ni fut son ber - ceau. Le ciel
see thee rise, The True North strong and free; And
broad do - main, From East to West - ern sea! Thou
cresc.
- toire est une é - po - pé - e Des plus bril - lants ex - ploits.
a mar-qué sa car - riè - re Dans ce mon - de nou - veau.
stand on guard, O Can - a - da, We stand on guard for thee.
land of hope for all who toil! Thou True North strong and free!
cresc.

(CHORUS, S. A. T. B. ad lib. in English)
f
Et ta va - leur, de foi trem - pé - e,
Tou - jours gui - dé par sa lu - miè - re,
O Can - a - da! Glo - rious and free!
f
O Can - a - da!
f
Pro - té - ge - ra nos foy - ers et nos droits,
Il gar - de - ra l'hon - neur de son dra - peau,
We stand on guard, We stand on guard for thee,

ff
D.S.
Pro - té - ge - ra nos foy - ers et nos droits.
Il gar - de - ra l'hon - neur de son dra - peau.
O Can - a - da! We stand on guard for thee.
ff
D.S.
ff

3. *De son patron, précurseur du vrai Dieu,*
Il porte au front l'auréole de feu.
Ennemi de la tyrannie Mais plein de loyauté,
Il veut garder dans l'harmonie, Sa fière liberté;
Et par l'effort de son génie, Sur notre sol asseoir la vérité,
Sur notre sol asseoir la vérité.

4. *Amour sacré du trône et de l'autel,*
Remplis nos coeurs de ton souffle immortel!
Parmi les races étrangères, Notre guide est la loi:
Sachons être un peuple de frères, Sous le joug de la foi.
Et répétons, comme nos pères, Le cri vainqueur: "Pour le Christ et le roi,"
Le cri vainqueur: "Pour le Christ et le roi."

3. O Canada! Beneath thy shining skies
May stalwart sons and gentle maidens rise
To keep thee steadfast thro' the years
From East to Western sea,
Our own beloved native land,
Our True North strong and free!

4. Ruler supreme, Who hearest humble pray'r,
Hold our Dominion in Thy loving care.
Help us to find, O God, in Thee
A lasting rich reward,
As waiting for the better day,
We ever stand on guard.

CAYMAN ISLANDS

Beloved Isle Cayman

Words and Music by
LEILA E. ROSS (1886-1968)

Valse moderato
mf
p
O land of soft, fresh breez - es
A - way from noise of ci - ties,
When tired of all ex - cite - ment
p
And ver - dant trees so fair,
Their fret and car - king care,
And glam - 'rous world - ly care,

The 'beloved isle' can refer to any of the three islands–Grand Cayman, Cayman Brac or Little Cayman.

The song was written in 1930 and is now accepted as the National Song. The National Anthem is "God Save the Queen".

With the Cre - a - tor's glo - ry Re - flec - ted
With moon-beams' soft ca - ress - es, Un-checked by
How sweet thy shores to reach And find a
ev - 'ry - where, O sea of pal - est
ga - rish glare, Thy fruit with rar - est
wel - come there, And when comes on the
em - 'rald, Merg - ing to dark - est blue,
juic - es, A - bun - dant, rich and free,
sea - son Of peace, good will to man,
When - e'er my thoughts fly God - ward,
When sweet church bells are chim - ing,
'Tis then I love thee best of all,

I always think of you.
My fond heart yearns for thee.
Be-lov-ed Isle Cay-man.
CHORUS
mf
Dear, ver-dant is-land, set in blue Car-
ib-bean Sea,
I'm com-ing, com-ing
ve-ry soon,
O beau-tious isle, to thee.

Al - though I wan - dered far,
My heart en - shrines thee yet.
Home-land, fair
Cay - man Isle,
I can - not thee for -
1
2
get.
get.

CENTRAL AFRICAN EMPIRE

La Renaissance

Words by BARTHÉLEMY BOGANDA
Music by HERBERT PEPPER
Alla Marcia moderato
f
O Cen-tra-fri - que, ô berceau des Bantous!
Re - prends ton droit au res - pect, à la vie!
Long - temps sou - mis, long - temps bri - mé par tous,
Mais de ce jour bri - sant la ty - ran - nie.
Ped.

This National Anthem was adopted by the National Assembly on 25th May 1960.
The words are by the first President of the Central African Republic.
The country has now been renamed the Central African Empire
and the new National Anthem is not yet available.

Dans le tra - vail, l'ordre et la di - gni - té,
Tu re - con - quiers ton droit, ton u - ni - té,
Et pour fran - chir cette é - ta - pe nou - vel - le,
Ped.
Ped.
De nos an - cê - tres la voix nous ap - pel - le.
Ped.
Ped.

CHORUS
Au tra-vail dans l'ordre et la di-gni-té, Dans le res-pect du
(Xylophones)
droit dans l'u-ni-té, Bri-sant la mi-sè-re et la ty-ran-nie,
Brandissant l'e-ten-dard de la Pa-trie.
ff
Ped.

Translation by
T.M. CARTLEDGE

Oh! Central Africa, cradle of the Bantu!
Take up again your right to respect, to life!
Long subjugated, long scorned by all,
But, from today, breaking tyranny's hold.
Through work, order and dignity
You reconquer your rights, your unity,
And to take this new step
The voice of our ancestors calls us.

Chorus

To work! In order and dignity,
In the respect for rights and in unity,
Breaking poverty and tyranny,
Holding high the flag of the Fatherland.

CHAD

La Tchadienne

Words by
Father GIDROL, S.J. and
students of St. Paul's School★

Music by
Father VILLARD, A.J.,
Arr. by Col. P. DUPONT

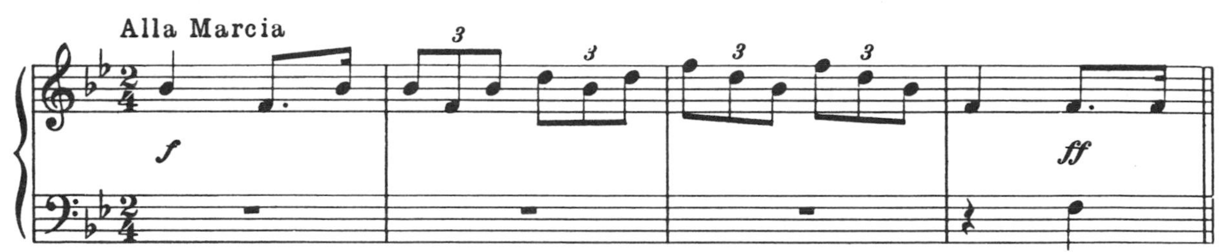
Alla Marcia
3
f
ff

Chorus
ff
Peu - ple Tcha-dien, de - bout et à l'ou-vra - ge! Tu as con-

- quis ta terre et ton droit; Ta li - ber - té naî-

★St. Paul's School at Fort Archambault trains teachers for Catholic education in Chad.

Fine
-tra de ton cou-ra - ge. Lè - ve les yeux, l'a-ve-nir est à Toi.
mf Verse
O mon Pa - ys,
mf
que Dieu te prenne en gar - - de,
Que tes voi - sins ad-mi-rent tes en-fants. Jo -
f
f

yeux, pa - ci - fique, a - vance en - chan - tant, Fi - dèle à tes an -
ciens qui te re - gar - - - dent.
Ped.

English Translation
by T.M.Cartledge

CHORUS

People of Chad, arise and take up the task!
You have conquered the soil and your rights;
Your freedom will be born of your courage.
Lift up your eyes, the future is yours.

VERSE

Oh, my Country, may God protect you,
May your neighbours admire your children.
Joyful, peaceful, advance as you sing,
Faithful to your fathers who are watching you.

Repeat Chorus

CHILE

Words by EUSEBIO LILLO (1826-1910) with modifications by FABIO PETRIS (1907) and ENRIQUE SORO (1909)

Music by RAMÓN CARNICER (1789-1855)

Music was adopted 17 September 1847. The date of the words was 12 August 1909 and it was recognised officially as the National Anthem on 27 June 1941. There are 5 verses; the fifth verse is that usually sung (as given here)

Chi - le es tu cie - lo a - zu - la - - - do pu - ras
Chi - le, thy skies spread a - bove thee, So
bri - sas te cru - zan tam - bién, y tu
sweet are the breez - es that roam O'er thy
cam - po de flo - res bor - da - - - do es la
fields rich - ly broi - dered with flow - er - lets That
co - pia fe - liz del E - dén. Ma - ges -
an - gels might make thee their home! Grand - ly

-tuo - sa es la blan - ca mon - ta - - - ña que te
ri - ses the snow - cov - ered moun - - - tain The
dió por ba - luar - te el Se - ñor, que te
ram - part be - stowed by the Lord, The
dió por ba - luar - te el Se - ñor, y e - se
ram - part be stowed by the Lord, And the
mar que tran - qui - lo te ba - ña te pro -
sea like a tran - quil foun - tain Of thy
p
p
p
p
p
3
3

mf
- me - te fu - tu - ro es - plen - dor. y e - se
fu - ture whis - pers its word. And the
mf
mar que tranqui - lo te ba - ña te pro -
sea like a tran - quil foun - tain Of thy
- me - te fu - tu - ro es - plen - dor.
fu - ture whis - pers its word.
CHORUS
f
Dul - - - ce Pa - - - tria, re -
Dear Home - - - land ac -
f

-ci - - - be los vo - tos
-cept the vows
con que Chi - - - le en tus
On thine al - - - - tars that
a - - - ras ju - ró que o la
Chi - - - - le shall be A
tum - ba se - rá de los li - bres o el a -
re - fuge from for - eign op - pres - sion Or the

-si - lo con-tra la o - pre - sión que o la
glo - rious home of the free! A
tum - ba se - rá de los li - - - bres o el a -
re - fuge from for - eign op - pres - - - sion Or the
-si - lo con-tra la o - pre - sión que o la tum - ba se -
glo - rious home of the free, A re - fuge from
rá de los li - bres o el a -
for - - - eign op - pres - sion Or the

-si - lo con-tra la o - pre - sión o el a-
glo - rious home of the free! Or the
-si - lo con-tra la o - pre - sión o el a-
glo - rious home of the free! Or the
-si - lo con-tra la o - pre - sión.
glo - rious home of the free!
ff

CHINA

People's Republic of China

Words by T'IEN HAN

Music by NIE ERH

3
3
3
3
Ch'i Lai! Bu yuan dzo nu - li - ti ren men! Bah wo - men - ti
A - rise! Ye who re - fuse to be bond slaves! With our ver - y
hsueh ro Dzo ch'en wo - men hsin - ti ch'ang ch'eng! Chung - hua min - chu
flesh and blood Let us build our new Great Wall! Chi - na's mass - es

This song was written in 1932. On 27th September 1949 it was officially approved as the National Anthem.
These words are no longer sung.
At the time of publication new words had been announced, but were not available.

daoliao dzwei weihsienti hsur - ho.
have met the day of ___ dan - ger;
Mei - go ren bei p'o chou fah - ch'u
Hate and an - ger fill the heart of
dzwei-ho-ti ho - sheng:
all of our coun - try - men.
Ch'i Lai! Ch'i Lai! Ch'i Lai!
A - rise! A - rise! A - rise!
Wo - men wan-chung ee - hsin
Man - y hearts with one mind
mao chou dee-run-ti p'ao - ho.
Brave the en - e - my gun - fire.
Ch'ien ching!
March on!
Mao chou dee-run-ti p'ao - ho.
Brave the en - e - my gun - fire.
Ch'ien ching! Ch'ien ching! Ch'ien ching! Ching!
March on! March on! March on! On!
3

CHINA
(TAIWAN)
Republic of China

Words based on a speech by
Dr. SUN YAT SEN (1867-1925)
Translated by
TU T'ING-HSIU

Music by
CHE'NG MAO-YÜN (1928)
Arr. by
Professor HUANG CHIH

Maestoso
mf
San min chu I, wo tang so
"San min chu I," our aim shall
chung, I kien min kuo, I chin - ta
be, To found a free land, world peace be our
rit.
tung. Tze erh to shih, wei min chien feng, su
stand. Lead on com - rades, van - guards ye are, Hold
a tempo
p a tempo
mf

Adopted as the National Anthem in 1929
The words 'San Min Chu I' express Dr. Sun's political philosophy of the Three People's Principles, i.e. government of the people, by the people, and for the people.

f
yeh fei shieh, chu I shih tsung, shih ching shih
fast your aim, by sun and star, Be earn - est and
f
yung, pi shing pi chung, I
brave, your coun - try to save, One
ff
ff
hsin I teh, kuan cheh shih chung!
heart, one soul, one mind one goal!

COLOMBIA

Words by
RAFAEL NUÑEZ
(1825-1894)

Music by
ORESTES SÍNDICI

This anthem was sung for the first time c. 1905. Rafael Nuñez was elected President of Colombia four times.

cresc.
sur - cos de do - lo - res El bien ger - mi - na
cresc.
f
ya, El bien ger - mi - na ya.
f
ff
¡Oh glo - ria in-mar-ce-
ff
- si - ble! ¡Oh jú - bi-lo in-mor-tal!
mf
En
cresc.
Fine
sur-cos de do - lo-res El bien ger - mi - na ya.
mf
cresc.
Fine

VERSE
p
1. Ce - só la ho-rri - ble no - che, La li - ber-tad su -
- bli - me De - rra - ma las au - ro - ras
De su in-ven-ci - ble luz. La hu - ma - ni-dad en -
- te - ra, Que en - tre ca-de - nas gi - me, Com -
mf
cresc.
f

D.C.
-pren - de las pa-la - bras Del que murió en la Cruz.
f
D.C.

2. *INDEPENDENCIA grita*
El mundo americano;
Se baña en sangre de héroes
La tierra de Colón.
Pero este gran principio:
EL REY NO ES SOBERANO,
Resuena, y los que sufren
Bendicen su pasión.

CHORUS

Oh unfading glory!
Oh immortal joy!
In furrows of pain
Good is already germinating.

1. The fearful night came to an end,
Liberty sublime
Is spreading the dawns
Of its invincible light.
The whole of humanity,
Which is groaning under chains,
Understands the words
Of the One who died on the Cross.

2. INDEPENDENCE cries
The American world;
In heroes' blood is bathing
The Land of Columbus.
But this great principle:
THE KING IS NOT SOVEREIGN,
Resounds, and those who suffer
Praise the passion in it.

CONGO
People's Republic of Congo

Words and Melody by
JEAN ROYER
JACQUES TONDRA
JO SPADILIERE

Arr. by HENRY COLEMAN

Maestoso
1. En ce jour le so-leil se lè - ve Et no-tre Con-go res-plen-dit. U-ne lon-gue nuit s'a-chè-ve, Un grand bon-heur a sur-gi. Chan-tons tous a-vec i-vres-se le chant de la li-ber-té.
2. Des fo-rêts jus-qu'à la sa-va - ne, Des sa-va-nes jus-qu'à la mer, Un seul peuple, u-ne seule â-me, Un seul cœur, ar-dent et fier. Lut-tons tous, tant que nous som-mes, pour no-tre vieux pa-ys noir.

CHORUS
p
Con - go-lais, de - bout fiè - re-ment par - tout, Pro-cla-mons l'u - nion de no-
p
-tre na - tion, Ou-bli - ons ce qui nous di - vi - se, so-yons
f
f
plus u - nis que ja - mais, Vi-vons pour no - tre de -
ff
ff
-vi - se: U - ni - té, tra - vail, pro - grès! Vi-vons

allargando
(3a volta)
pour no - tre de - vi - se: U - ni - té, tra - vail, pro - grès!
allargando

3. *Et s'il nous faut mourir, en somme*
Qu'importe puisque nos enfants,
Partout, pourront dire comme
On triomphe en combattant,
Et dans le moindre village
Chantent sous nos trois couleurs.

Translation by T. M. Cartledge

1. On this day the sun rises
And our Congo stands resplendent.
A long night is ended,
A great happiness has come.
Let us all, with wild joyfulness, sing
The song of freedom.

CHORUS Arise, Congolese, proud every man,
Proclaim the unity of our nation.
Let us forget what divides us
And become more united than ever.
Let us live our motto:
Unity, work, progress.
Let us live our motto:
Unity, work, progress.

2. From the forest to the bush,
From the bush to the ocean,
One people, one soul,
One heart, ardent and proud.
Let us all fight, every one of us,
For our old black country.

3. And if we have to die,
What does it really matter? Our children
Everywhere will be able to say how
Triumph comes through battle,
And in the smallest village
Sing beneath our three colours.

COSTA RICA

Words by
JOSÉ MARIA ZELEDÓN (b. 1877)
English verses by
MARY ELIZABETH and DICCON SHAW

Music by
MANUEL MARÍA GUTIÉRREZ
(1829-1887)

Allegro Marcial
ff
f
No - ble pa - tria tu hermo - sa ban-de - ra ex - pre-
No - ble coun - try, the life of your peo - ple Is re-
f
- sión de tu vi - da nos da: ba-jo el lím - pi-do a-zul de tu
- veal'd in the flag that you fly; For in peace, white and pure, they live

Adopted as the National Anthem in 1853, when composed.
The first two verses allude to the national flag, of which the colours are blue, white and red.
They were chosen as the result of a public competition in 1900.

cie - lo blan-ca y pu - ra des-can - sa la paz.
tran - quil 'Neath the clear lim - pid blue of your sky.
En la lu - cha te - naz de fe - cun - da la - bor que en - ro -
And their fa - ces are rud - dy with ar - du - ous toil In the
- je - ce del hom - bre la faz, con - qui - sta - ron tus
fields 'neath the life - giv - ing sun. Though your sons are but
hi - jos - la-brie - gos sen-ci - llos— e-ter - no pres - ti - gio, es-ti - ma y ho -
pea - sants, their la - bours e - ter - nal Es-teem,— re - nown,— and hon - our have

-nor e - ter - no pres - ti - gio, es - ti - ma y ho - nor.
won, es - teem, re - nown, and hon - our have won.
pp
¡Sal-ve, oh tie - rra gen - til! ¡Sal-ve, oh ma - dre de a-
Hail, oh land of our birth! gra-cious land that we
pp
ff
-mor! Cuan-do al - gu - no pre - ten - da tu glo - ria man-
love! If an en - e - my seek - ing to slan - der you,
ff
-char, ve - rás a tu pue - blo, va - lien - te y vi -
harms Your name, then we will a - ban - don our
p
p

- ril, la tos - ca he - rra - mien - ta en ar - ma tro -
farms And a - rise with fer - vour to take up our
ff
- car. ¡Sal-ve, oh pa - tria! tu pró - di - go sue - lo dul - ce a -
arms. O sweet coun - try, our re - fuge and shel - ter; How
ff
- bri - go y sus-ten - to nos da; ba - jo el lím - pi - do a-zul de tu
fer - tile your life - giv - ing soil! May your peo - ple, con-tent - ed and
rall.
cie - lo ¡vi - van siem pre el tra-ba - jo y la paz!
peace - ful, Un - mo - lest - ed con - tin - ue their toil.
rall.

CUBA

La Bayamesa

Translated by
G. H. HATCHMAN

Versified by
MARTIN SHAW

Words and Music by
PEDRO FIGUEREDO
(1819-1870)

Tempo di Marcia
Al com-ba - te co-rred, ba - ya-
Swift, oh men of Ba-ya - mo, to

Sung for the first time in 1868 during the battle of Bayamo, in which Figueredo played a leading part.

-me - - ses que la Pa - tria os con - tem - pla or - gu -
bat - - tle! Proud - ly watch - ing, your Moth - er - land ac -
cresc.
-llo - - sa; no te - máis u - na muer - te glo -
-cepts you. Fear not fight - ing to fall; glo - ry
cresc.
-rio - - - sa, que mo - rir por la
waits you! For your coun - try to
pp cresc.
Pa - tria es vi - vir. En ca -
die, is to live. To sub -
ff
pp cresc.

-de - nas vi - vir, es vi - vir en a -
-mit to the bon - dage of a - - - - liens Is to
-fren - ta y o - pro - bio su - mi - do; del cla -
suf - fer a life of de - gra - da - - - - tion. Hark! the
cresc.
cresc.
-rín es - cu - chad el so - ni - - - - do; ¡a las
trum - pet is call - ing your na - - - - tion! Va - liant
ar - mas, va - lien - tes, co - rred! En ca -
he - roes, "To arms!" be your cry. To sub -
1
2
pp
pp

CZECHOSLOVAKIA

Part I: Kde Domov Můj?

Words by
JOSEF KAJETÁN TYL
(1808-1856)

Music by
FRANTIŠEK SAN ŠKROUP,
(1801-1862)

This State hymn was officially recognised as the National Anthem in 1919. It is in two parts. The first is Czech and the second is a Slovak folksong commemorating the exodus of Slovak students from Bratislavia in 1843.

mf cresc. f
ráj ___ to na po-hled! A to je ta krá - sná ze - mě, ze-mě
mf
cresc.
f

če - ská do-mov můj, __ ze-mě če - ská do-mov můj!

Part 2: Nad Tatrú sa blýská

Words by
JANKO MATÚSKA (1821-1877)

Traditional Melody

Allegro energico

mf

Nad Ta - trú sa blý - ská, hro - my di - vo bi - jú,

mf

nad Ta - trú sa blý - ská, hro - my di - vo bi - jú.

Part 1

Where is my home, where is my home?
Streams are rushing through the meadows,
'Mid the rocks sigh fragrant pine groves,
Orchards decked in Spring's array
Scenes of Paradise portray.
And this land of wond'rous beauty
Is the Czech land, home of mine,
Is the Czech land, home of mine.

Part 2

Lightning strikes our mighty Tatra tempest-shaken,
Lightning strikes our mighty Tatra tempest-shaken.
Stand we fast, friends of mine,
Storms must pass, sun will shine,
Slovaks shall awaken.

DENMARK

Kong Kristian

Words by
JOHANNES EWALD (1743-1781)
English versification by
H.W. LONGFELLOW
(1807-1882)

Music by
D.L.ROGERT (?)
(1742-1813)
This is not certain.

Maestoso
f
★ Kong Kri - stian stod ved høj - en Mast i røg og
King Christ - ian stood by the loft - y mast In mist and
f

damp. Hans vær - ge ham - re - de så fast, at
smoke; His sword was ham - mer - ing so fast, Through

go - tens hjælm og hjer - ne brast; da sank hver fjendt - ligt
Go - thic helm and brain it passed; Then sank each hos - tile

This is the official National and Royal Anthem. Music first appeared in ms. form c.1762-1777; words first used in the ballad opera *The Fishermen* 1780. There are other verses.

★ King Christian IV (1577-1648) was one of Denmark's great patriotic leaders.

mf
spejl og — mast i røg og damp. "Fly," skreg de, "fly, hvad
hulk and mast In mist and smoke. "Fly!" shout-ed they, "fly,
mf

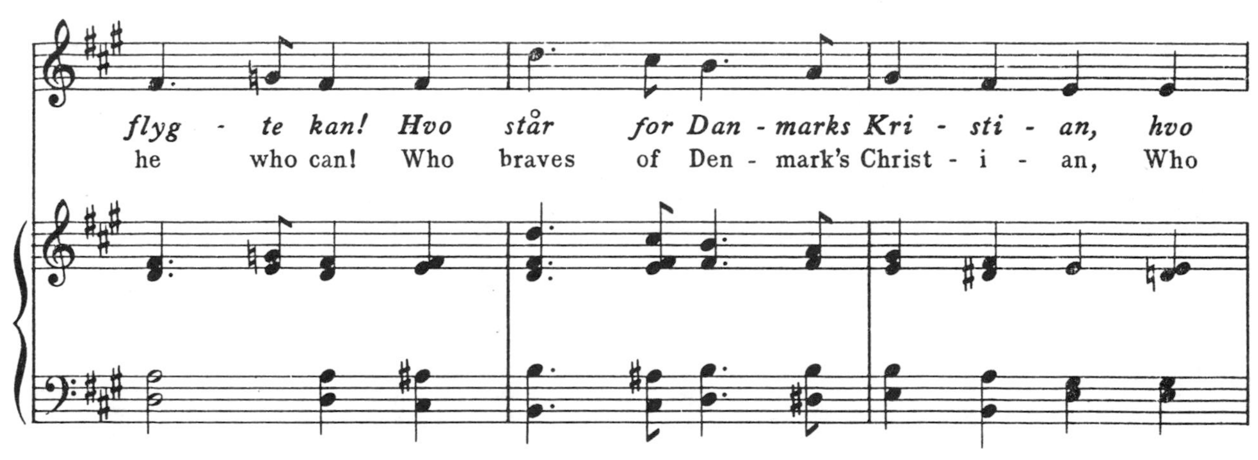
flyg - te kan! Hvo står for Dan - marks Kri - sti - an, hvo
he who can! Who braves of Den - mark's Christ - i - an, Who

cresc.
f
står for Dan - marks Kri - sti - an i kamp?"
braves of Den - mark's Christ - i - an The stroke?"
cresc.
f

DENMARK

Der er et yndigt land

Words by
ADAM GOTTLOB OEHLENSCHLÄGER (1779-1850)
Translated by
CHARLES BRATLI

Music by
HANS ERNST KRØYER
(1798-1879)

Moderato
f
Der er et yn - digt land, det
I know a love - ly land, Whose
f

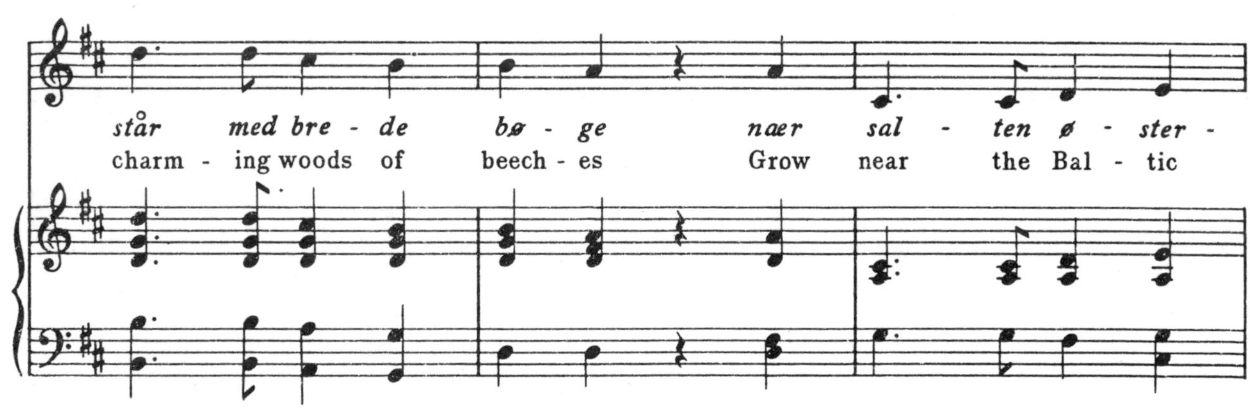
står med bre - de bø - ge nær sal - ten ø - ster -
charm - ing woods of beech - es Grow near the Bal - tic

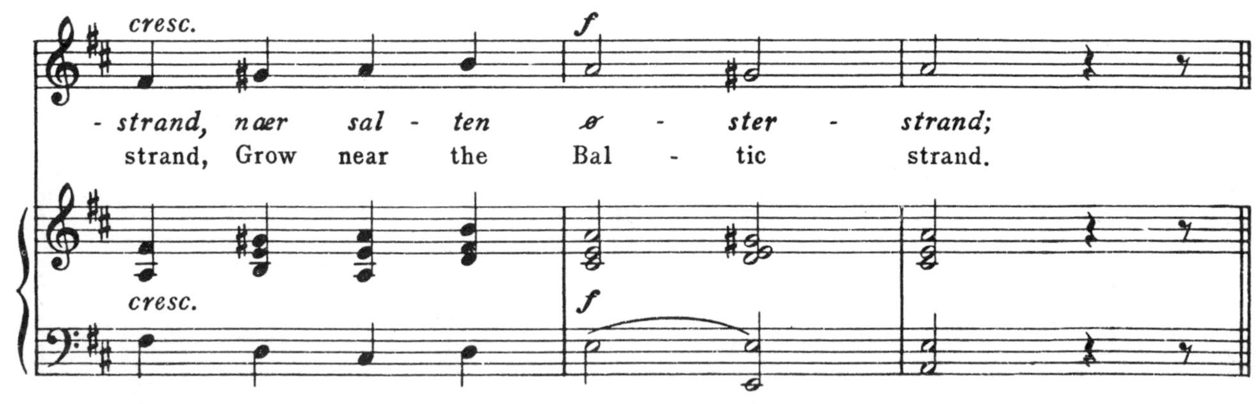
cresc.
f
- strand, nær sal - ten ø - ster - strand;
strand, Grow near the Bal - tic strand.
cresc.
f

Also used on national occasions. Written c. 1819. Its popularity as a national song dates from 4th July, 1844, when students sang it at a national festal meeting to a gathering of 12,000 Danes.

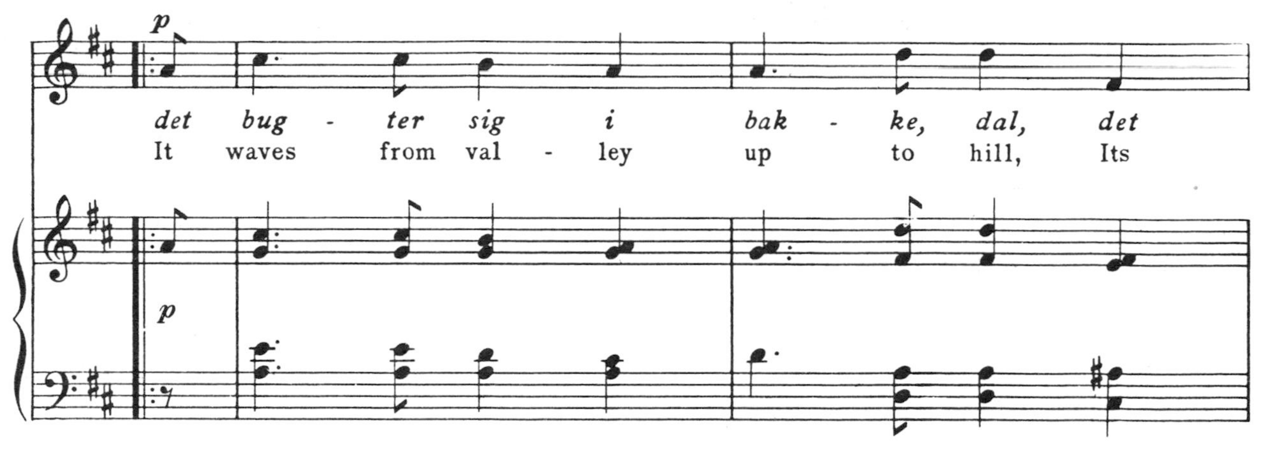
p
det bug - ter sig i bak - ke, dal, det
It waves from val - ley up to hill, Its
p

cresc.
f
p
hed - der gam - le Dan - mark, og det er Frej - as
name is old - en Den - mark, And here dwells Frey - a
cresc.
f
p

f
sal, og det er Frej - - as sal.
still, And here dwells Frey - - a still.
f

DOMINICAN REPUBLIC

Words by
EMILIO PRUD'HOMME
English versification by
J. E. HALES and
MARY ELIZABETH SHAW

Music by
JOSÉ REYÉS (1835-1905)

Marziale
Quis-que-ya-nos va-lien-tes, al-ce-mos nues-tro can-to con vi-va e-mo-ción, Y del
Va-liant sons of Quis-que-ya, our chor-us, Let us, heart-felt and strong, sing to the world; While, de-

First sung as National Anthem in 1900. Quisqueya is the native name of the island of Santo Domingo.

mun - do a la faz os - ten - te - mos nues-tro in-vic - to glo-rio - so pen-
- fi - ant and daunt - less, be - fore us We will flou - rish our stan - dard un-
p
- dón. ¡Sal - ve el pue - blo que in tré - pi - do y fuer - te, a la
furled. Hail! O peo - ple in - tre - pid and dar - ing, Who with
gue - rra a mo-rir se lan - zó. Cuan-do en bé - li - co re - to de
ea - ger - ness sprang to at - tack; And, of blood-shed and dan - ger un-
muer - te sus ca - de - nas de es - cla - vo rom -
- car - ing, Saw the fet - ters of sla - ve - ry

-pió.
crack.
f
p
pp
f
Nin-gun pue-blo ser li-bre me-
Un-de-serv-ing of free-dom the
-re-ce si es es-cla-vo in do-len-te y ser-vil: Si en su
na-tion Which in ty-ran-ny's bond tame-ly lives, And is
pe-cho la lla-ma no cre-ce que tem-
lack-ing the fine in-spi-ra-tion That from
f
f

-pló el he-ro-is-mo vi-ril. Mas Quis-que-ya la in-dó-mi-ta y
true vi-rile cour-age de-rives. But the sons of Quis-que-ya ne'er
bra-va Siem-pre al-ti-va la fren-te al-za-
fail her, And her head car-ried high shall re-
-rá: Que si fue-re mil ve-ces es-
-main; Though a thou-sand times foes should as-
-cla-va Otras tan-tas ser li-bre sa-brá.
-sail her, She her free-dom would e-ver re-gain.

ECUADOR

Words by
JUAN LEÓN MERA
(1832-1894)
English versification by
T. M. CARTLEDGE

Music by
ANTONIO NEUMANE
(1818-1871)

Officially recognized as the National Anthem by a government decree in 1948.
It had been in use for a considerable time before. The author, in his later years, was President of the Senate of Ecuador.

CHORUS
¡Sal - ve, Oh Pa - tria, mil ve - ces! ¡Oh
We sa - lute e'er a - gain this our
Pa - tria, Glo - ria á ti! Glo - ria á
home - land, Glo - ry be to
ti! Ya tu pe - cho, tu pe - cho re - bo - sa Go - zo y
you, Joy and peace, your rad - iance be - stow - ing, Who, ex-
paz, ya tu pe - cho re - bo - sa; y tu
- ceed - ing the sun, bright - ly shine. We sa -

cresc.
fren - te, tu fren - te ra - dio - sa Mas que el
-lute e'er a-gain this our home - land, Glo - ry
p
cresc.
sol con - tem-pla - mos lu - cir, y tu
be to you, your breast o'er - flow - ing, Joy and
f
cresc.
fren - te, tu fren - te ra - dio - sa Mas que el
peace, your rad - iance be - stow - ing, Who ex -
1
2
Fine
sol con-tem-pla - mos lu - cir. y tu cir.
-ceed - ing the sun, bright - ly shine. We sa - shine.

VERSE
p
Los pri - mo - ros los hi - jos del sue - lo que so -
Com - ing first were the sons_ of the coun - try Which Pi -
pp
- ber - bio, el Pi - chin - cha de - co - ra Te a - cla -
- chin - cha on high is a - dorn - ing, Who ac -
- ma - ron por siem - pre_ se - ño - ra Y ver -
- claimed you as their sov' - reign_ la - dy And shed -
- tie - ron su san - gre por ti Dios mi -
blood for the sake of the land: God look'd
p

ró y a - cep - tó el ho - lo - ca - us - to Y e - sa,
on and ac - cept - ed the sa - cri - fice, And that
san - gre fue ger - men fe - cun - do De o - tros
blood was seed pro - li - fic; Oth - er
hé - roes que a - tó - ni - to el mun - do Vió en tu
her - oes the world ob - served, as - tound - ed, For the
f

1
tor - no a mi - lla - res sur - gir. Dios mi -
fight rise___ up - on ev - 'ry hand. God look'd
1
2
- gir. a mi - lla - res sur -
hand, rise___ up - on ev - 'ry
2
ff
f
- gir, a mi - lla - res sur - gir.
hand, rise up - on ev - 'ry hand.
D.𝄋 al Fine
D.𝄋 al Fine
pp
f

EGYPT

Arab Republic of Egypt

Words by
SALAH SHAHYN

Music by
KAMAL ATTAWYL

This was a song which achieved great national popularity in 1956.
The National Anthem was derived from it, and first used on 20th May, 1960.
The chorus only is sung, followed by an instrumental interlude, then a repeat of the chorus.

mf
mf
f
f
Wal - la Za-man Ya Si - la - hi
Ish - taq-ti Lak Fi Ki - fa - hi
In - taq We Qul A - na
Sa - hi
Ya Har - b Wal - la Za - man.
sf

Transliteration

1. *Walla Zaman 'Algunud*
Zahfa Bitir'id Ri'ud
Halfa Tiruh Lam Ti'ud
Illa Binasr Al-zaman.

2. *Hummu Wu Dummu Al-sufuf*
Shilu Al-hayat 'Alkufuf
Yama Al-'adu Rah Yishuf
Minkum Binar El-fida.

3. *Ya Magd Ya Magdina*
Yalli Itbanait 'Andana
Bishaqana Wa Kaddina
'Umrak Ma Tibqa Hawan.

4. *Masr Al-hurra Min Yihmiha*
Nihmiha Bislahna
Ardh Al-thawra Min Yifdiha
Nifdiha Biarwahna.

5. *Al-sha'b Biyizhaf Zayy El-nur*
Al sha'b Gebal Al-sha'b Bhur
Burkan Ghadban Burkan Biyfur
Zilzal Biyshuqq Lohom Fi Qbur.

Free Translation

Chorus O! my weapon!
How I long to clutch thee!
Respond, awake and alert,
For valiant combat.

1. Hail, gallant troops,
Dashing with thunderous roar,
Swearing never to return
Except with epoch-making victory.

2. Rise and raise a host,
With loyal hearts ready for sacrifice.
Oh! the horror the enemy shall suffer
Through the fire of your zeal.

3. O! glory of our Country,
Achieved with our own efforts alone,
By hard hours of toil,
Never to be wasted or endangered.

4. Who shall protect Free Egypt?
We shall protect it with our lives.
Land of the Revolution, who will sacrifice for her sake?
We will, with our lives.

5. The people advance like the light,
The people stand like mountains and seas,
Angry volcanoes, erupting volcanoes,
Earthquakes digging graves for the enemy.

EL SALVADOR

Words by
JUAN J. CAÑAS (1826-1918)
English versification by
MARY ELIZABETH
AND DICCON SHAW

Music by
JUAN ABERLE
(1846-1930)

This was written in 1879 and adopted as the National Anthem in 1953
General Juan Cañas was a diplomat and soldier; at one time Minister of Foreign Affairs.

su - yos po-der - nos lla - mar Y ju -
name of thy chil - dren we bear, And with
- re - mos la vi - da a - ni - mo - sos Sin des -
bold and un-tir - ing de - vo - tion To thy
can - so a su bien con - sa - grar.
ser - vice our lives let us swear.
f
Sa - lu -
Moth - er
f

-de - mos la Pa - tria or - gu - llo - sos De hi - jos
coun - try, thy peo - ple sa - lute thee! Proud - ly the
su - llos po-der - nos lla-mar Y ju -
name of thy chil - dren we bear, And with
-re - mos la vi - da a - ni - mo - sos Sin des -
bold and un-tir - ing de - vo - tion to thy
-can - so a su bien con - sa - grar
ser - vice our lives let us swear.
f

f
con - sa - grar
Our lives we swear,
con - sa - grar con - sa -
Our lives we swear, Our lives we
- grar con - sa - grar
swear, Our lives we swear.
sf
sf
Fine
p
VERSE
1. De la paz en la di-cha su -
1. Peace, con - tent - ment, and hap-pi-ness
Fine
p

- pre - ma Siem-pre no - ble so-ñó El Sal-va dor Fué ob-te-
ev - er Was the con-stant dream of El Sal - va - dor; To a-
- ner - - - la su e-ter-no pro-ble - - - - ma, Con-ser-
- chieve it was her glor-ious am - bi - - - - tion, And to
- var - la es su glo - ria ma - yor. Y con
keep it for ev - - - - er - more. For with
fé in-que - bran-ta - ble el ca - mi - no Del pro-
ea - ger faith which nev - er shall fal - ter Towards the

-gre - so se a-fa - na en se-guir en se-guir Por lle-
bright star of pro - gress she fol - lows the way; To se-
-nar su gran-dio - so des-ti - no, Con-quis-
-cure for her-self a hap - py fu - ture, And her
-tar - se un fe-liz por-ve-nir Le pro-
des - ti-ny glo - rious o-bey. The at-
-te - - - je u-na fé-rrea ba-rre - ra Con-tra el
-tack of a vil-lain-ours trai - tor Her

cho - - - que de ruin des-leal-tad Des-de el
ram part of steel has with-stood Since the
dí - - - a que en su alta ban-de - - - ra Con su
day when a-loft on her stan - - - dard She wrote
san - gre es-cri-bió li-ber-tad! es-cri-bió li-ber-
"Free - dom" in let - ters of blood She wrote "Free - dom" in
tad! es-cri-bió li-ber-tad!
let - ters, in let - ters of blood.
D.C. al Fine
D.C. al Fine

CORO *Saludemos la patria orgullosos*
De Hijos suyos podernos llamar;
Y juremos la vida animosos,
Sin descanso a su bien consagrar.

2. *Libertad es su dogma, es su guia,*
Que mil veces logró defender;
Y otras tantas de audaz tirania
Rechazar el odioso poder.
Dolorosa y sangrienta es su historia,
Pero excelsa y brillante a la vez,
Manantial de legitima gloria,
Gran lección de espartana altivez.
No desmaya su innata bravura:
En cada hombre hay un héroe inmortal,
Que sabrá mantenerse a la altura
De su antiguo valor proverbial.

3. *Todos son abnegados y fieles*
Al prestigio del bélico ardor,
Con que siempre segaron laureles
De la Patria salvando el honor.
Respetar los derechos extraños
Y apoyarse en la recta razón
Es para ella, sin torpes amaños,
La invariable, más firme ambición.
Y en seguir esta linea se aferra,
Dedicando su esfuerzo tenaz
En hacer cruda guerra a la guerra;
Su ventura se encuentra en la paz.

CHORUS Mother country, thy people salute thee!
Proudly the name of thy children we bear,
And with bold and untiring devotion
To thy service our lives let us swear.

2. Never tiring, her people have battled
To preserve and guard their liberty:
And with valour have a thousand times over
Broken the powers of base tyranny.
For, though brilliant and sublime is her story,
Yet it tells of her blood and her suffering beside,
And in this is revealed her true glory
And her noble and stoical pride.
All her sons shall be heroes immortal;
They are daring, resourceful, and bold;
For their bravery is a tradition
And they fight like their fathers of old.

3. They will follow this ancient tradition
Which has won for them undying fame
Since with ardour, self-denying and faithful,
They kept spotless their Motherland's name.
Her ambition is firm and unchanging,
To respect and observe others' rights is her pride;
To maintain ever pure the fount of justice
Where uprightness and trust are allied.
She will follow this path with devotion
And with courage which never shall cease;
For, although she gives battle for battle,
Her most fervent desire is for peace.

EQUATORIAL GUINEA

Music
Arr. by W. L. REED

Became fully independent 12 October 1968.

3
3
3
3
3
ff
(rit.)

ESTONIA

Words by
JOHANN WOLDEMAR JANSSEN (1819-1900)

Music by
FREDRIK PACIUS (1809-1891)
Arr. by
HENRY COLEMAN

Maestoso con entusiasmo

f

Mu i - sa - maa, mu õnn ja rõõm, Kui

kau - nis o - led sa! Ei lei - a mi - na

mf

ii - al teal See suu - re lai - a il - ma peal, Mis

ff

mull' nii ar - mas o - leks ka Kui sa mu i - sa - maa!

First acknowledged as Estonia's National Anthem c.1917. Sung for first time at National Singing Festival, 1st July, 1869
The tune is the same as that of Finland's National Anthem.
The National Anthem of the U.S.S.R. is now used inside Estonia.

2. *Sa oled mind ju sünnitand*
Ja üles kasvatand;
Sind tänan mina alati
Ja jään sul truuks surmani!
Mul kõige armsam oled sa,
Mu kallis isamaa!

3. *Su üle Jumal valvaku,*
Mu armas isamaa!
Ta olgu sinu kaitseja
Ja võtku rohkest' õnnista'
Mis iial ette võtad sa,
Mu kallis isamaa!

Translation by Jenny Wahl

1. My native land, my joy, delight,
How fair thou art and bright;
And nowhere in the world all round
Can ever such a place be found
So well beloved as I love thee,
My native country dear!

2. My little cradle stood on thy soil,
Whose blessings ease my toil.
With my last breath my thanks to thee,
For true to death I'll ever be
O worthy, most beloved and fine,
Thou, dearest country mine!

3. May God in Heaven thee defend,
My best, my dearest land!
May He be guard, may He be shield,
For ever may He bless and wield
O graciously all deeds of thine,
Thou dearest country mine!

ETHIOPIA

Arranged and
Harmonised by
W. L. REED

First used on Revolution Day, September 1st 1975. Words not yet available.

3
3
3
3
p
rit. . . .
a tempo
f
rit. . . .
ff
a tempo
8va bassa...

FAROE ISLANDS

Tú alfagra land mítt

Words by
SÍMUN av SKARÐI (1872-1942)
English translation by
C.NISSEN
Music by
PETER ALBERG (1885-1940)
Arr. by HENRY COLEMAN
Moderato
1. Tú al - fagr - a land mítt, mín dýr - ast - a ogn! Á
vetr - i - so rand - hvítt, á sumr - i við logn, tú
tek - ur meg at tær, so tætt i tín favn. Tit

This became the National Anthem in the late 1930s.

oyggj - ar so mæt - ar, Gud sign - i tað navn, sum
menn tykk - um gov - u, tá teir tykk - um só - u, Ja,
Gud sign - i Føroy - ar, mitt land!

2. *Hin roðin, sum skínur*
á sumri í líð;
hin ódnin, sum týnir
mangt lív vetrartíð,
og myrkrið, sum fjalir
mær bjartasta mál,
og ljósið, sum spælir
mær sigur í sál:
alt streingir, ið tóna,
sum vága og vóna,
at eg verji Føroyar, mítt land!

3. *Eg nígi ti niður*
í bøn til tín, Gud:
Hin heilagi friður
mær falli í lut!
Lat sál mína tváa
sær í tíni dýrd!
So torir hon vága,
-av Gudi væl skírd-
at bera tað merki,
sum eyðkennir verkið,
ið varðveitir Føroyar, mítt land!

Free Translation

1. Oh, Faroe Islands, my dearest treasure!
When winter storms roar, in warm summer night,
You draw out yonder my home in your embrace.
You Islands so graceful, God bless the name
That our forefathers gave you when beyond the ocean they found you.
Yes, God bless the Faroe Islands, my land.

2. That sun gleam which hovers round summer green time
And the storm which claims so many a life in winter;
The darkness which hides my mountain range and peak
And the light which billows and whispers in the mind,
Are strings which vibrate and secretly compel me
To guard you, Faroe Islands, my country!

3. My knee I will bend in prayer to you, God,
Your peace, Oh Thou highest, as a message to me bring!
My soul will bow at your baptismal blessing
Then it may venture, I hope, with frankness and joy
To carry forward the mark which witnesses the task
That serves you, Faroe Islands, my land!

FIJI

Words by
M. PRESCOTT

Harmonisation as used by
Royal Fiji Police Band

mf
Bless - ing grant, oh God of na - tions, on the isles of Fi - ji,
Bless - ing grant, oh God of na - tions, on the isles of Fi - ji,
mf
As we stand u - ni - ted un - der no - ble ban - ner blue.
Shores of gold - en sand and sun - shine, hap - pi - ness and song.
mf
And we hon - our and de - fend the cause of free - dom ev - er,
Stand u - ni - ted, we of Fi - ji, fame and glo - ry ev - er,
mf
REFRAIN
f
On - ward march to - geth - er, God bless Fi - ji!
On - ward march to - geth - er, God bless Fi - ji!
For
f

The main anthem is that of Great Britain.
This national song is sung after 'God Save the Queen'.
Fiji became an independent Commonwealth country 10 October 1970

Fi - ji, ev - er Fi - ji, let our voi - ces ring with pride, For

Fi - ji, ev - er Fi - ji, her name hail far and wide, A land of

free - dom, hope and glo - ry to en - dure what - e'er be - fall. May God bless

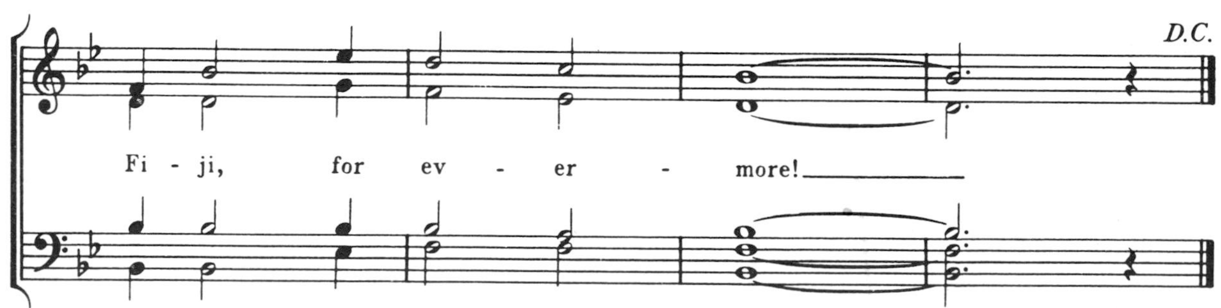
D.C.
Fi - ji, for ev - er - more!

FINLAND

Maamme laulu

OUR LAND

Words by
JOHAN LUDVIG RUNEBERG (1804-1877)
Translated by
CHARLES WHARTON STORK

Music by
FREDRIK PACIUS (1809-1891)

Andante maestoso
f
1. Oi Maam - me, Suo - - mi, syn - nyin -
1. Our land, our land, our na - tive
f

- maa! Soi sa - na kul - tai - nen!
land, Oh, let her name ring clear!

mf
Ei laak - so - a, ei kuk - ku - laa, Ei
No peaks a - gainst the heav'ns that stand, No
mf

This Anthem was written by Finland's National Poet in 1846
Sung for the first time at a students' gathering, 13th May 1848.

cresc.
vet - tä, ran - taa rak-kaam-paa, Kuin ko - ti-maa tää poh-joi -
gen - tle dales or foam-ing strand are lov'd as we our home re -
cresc.
ff
- nen, Maa kal - lis i - si - en!
- vere, The earth our sires held dear.
ff

2. *Sun kukoistukses kuorestaan*
Kerrankin puhkeaa!
Viel' lempemme saa nousemaan
Sun toivos, riemus loistossaan,
Ja kerran laulus, synnyinmaa,
Korkeemman kaiun saa!

2. The flowers in their buds that grope
Shall burst their sheaths with spring;
So from our love to bloom shall ope
Thy gleam, thy glow, thy joy, thy hope,
And higher yet some day shall ring
The patriot song we sing!

FRANCE

La Marseillaise

English translation of first verse by
PERCY BYSSHE SHELLEY (1792-1822)
of second verse by
MARY ELIZABETH SHAW

Words and Music by
CLAUDE-JOSEPH ROUGET de L'ISLE
(1760 - 1836)

Alla marcia
f
1. Al-lons en-fants de la Pa - tri - e, Le jour de
1. Ye sons of France, a - wake to glo - ry, Hark, hark, what
f
gloire est ar - ri - vé. Con - tre nous, de la ty - ran-
my - riads bid you rise: Your child-ren, wives and grand - sires
Ped.
-ni - e, L'é - ten-dard sang - lant est le - vé, l'e - ten-
hoa - ry, ★See their tears and hear their cries, see their
ff
ff
Ped.

★Shelley has "behold"

Written and composed on 24th April, 1792, as a marching song.
Adopted as National Anthem, 15th July, 1795

p
dard_ sang-lant est le-vé. En-ten-dez-vous, dans les cam-
tears_ and hear their_ cries! Shall hateful ty-rants mis-chief_
p
cresc.
-pag-nes Mu-gir ces fa-rou-ches sol-dats. Ils
breed-ing With hire-ling_ hosts, a ruf-fian band Af-
cresc.
vien-nent jus-que dans nos bras é-gor-ger vos fils, vos com-
-fright and de-so-late the land, While peace and li-ber-ty lie
ff
-pag-nes. Aux ar-mes ci-toy-ens! For-
bleed-ing? To arms,_ to arms, ye brave! Th'a-
ff

- mez ___ vos ba-tail-lons, ___ Mar- chons, mar - chons!
- veng - ing sword un-sheathe! ___ March on! march on!

Qu'un sang im - pur ___ A - breu - ve nos sil-lons.
All hearts re - solved ___ on vic - to-ry or death.

D.C.

2. *Amour sacré de la Patrie,*
Conduis, soutiens nos bras vengeurs.
Liberté, liberté chérie,
Combats avec tes défenseurs; (bis)
Sous nos drapeaux, que la victoire
Accoure à tes mâles accents;
Que tes ennemis expirants
Voient ton triomphe et notre gloire!

* *Aux armes citoyens, etc.*

2. O sacred love of France, undying,
Th'avenging arm uphold and guide.
Thy defenders, death defying,
Fight with Freedom at their side.
Soon thy sons shall be victorious
When the banner high is raised;
And thy dying enemies, amazed,
Shall behold thy triumph, great and glorious.

To arms, to arms, ye brave! etc.

* **It is customary to repeat** ***'Aux armes citoyens'***

GABON

La Concorde

Words and Music by
GEORGES DAMAS
Arr. by HENRY COLEMAN

This became the National Anthem when Gabon achieved independence on 17th August 1960

vibre et nous sou-lè - ve! C'est en-fin notre es-sor vers la fé-
-li - ci - té. C'est en-fin notre es-sor vers la fé-li - ci - té.
rall 2nd time
Fine
Fine
CHORUS
p dolce
E - blou - is - sant et fier, le jour
p
su - bli-me monte Pour-chas - sant à ja-mais

— l'in - jus - tice et la hon - te. Qu'il mon -
- te, monte en - co - re et cal - me nos a -
- lar - mes, Qu'il pro - ne la ver - tu ——
— et re - pous - se les armes. ——

2 *Oui que le temps heureux rêvé par nos ancêtres*
Arrive enfin chez nous, rejouisse les êtres,
Et chasse les sorciers, ces perfides trompeurs
Qui semaient le poison et répandaient la peur.

3 *Afin qu'aux yeux du monde et des nations amies*
Le Gabon immortel reste digne d'envie,
Oublions nos querelles, ensemble bâtissons
L'édifice nouveau auquel tous nous rêvons.

4 *Des bords de l'Ocean au cœur de la forêt,*
Demeurons vigilants, sans faiblesse et sans haine!
Autour de ce drapeau, qui vers l'honneur nous mène,
Saluons la Patrie et chantons sans arrêt:

Translation by
T.M. CARTLEDGE

Chorus United in concord and brotherhood,
Awake, Gabon, dawn is at hand.
Stir up the spirit that thrills and inspires us!
At last we rise up to attain happiness.

1 Dazzling and proud, the sublime day dawns,
Dispelling for ever injustice and shame.
May it still advance and calm our fears,
May it promote virtue and banish warfare.

2 Yes, may the happy days of which our ancestors dreamed
Come for us at last, rejoicing our hearts,
And banish the sorcerers, those perfidious deceivers
Who sowed poison and spread fear.

3 So that, in the eyes of the world and of friendly nations,
The immortal Gabon may maintain her good repute,
Let us forget our quarrels, let us build together
The new structure of which we all have dreamed.

4 From the shores of the Ocean to the heart of the forest,
Let us remain vigilant, without weakness and without hatred!
Around this flag which leads us to honour,
Let us salute the Fatherland and ever sing:

THE GAMBIA

Words by
VIRGINIA JULIA HOWE (b. 1927)
Adapted by J. F. HOWE (b. 1929)
from the traditional Mandinka song
"Foday Kaba Dumbuya"
Broadly (♩ = 80)
f
For the Gam - bi - a, our___ home - land, We___
strive and work and pray, That all may_ live in u - ni - ty, Free -
- dom and peace each day. Let jus - tice guide our ac - tions To -
mp

Officially adopted 18 February 1965, when Gambia became independent.

-wards the com-mon good, And join our di-verse
peo-ples To prove man's bro-ther-hood. We
cresc.
pledge our firm al-le-giance, Our pro-mise we re-new; Keep
ff
us, great God of na-tions, To the Gam-bia ev-er true.
rall.

GERMANY (EAST)

Democratic Republic of Germany

Words by
JOHANNES R. BECHER (1891-1958)
English words by
YVONNE KAPP

Music by
HANNS EISLER (1898-1962)

f

1. Auf - er - stan - den aus Ru - i - nen und der Zu - kunft
1. From the ru - ins ris - en new - ly To the fu - ture

zu - ge - wandt, lass uns dir zum Gu - ten die - nen,
turned we stand. May we serve your good weal tru - ly,

Deutsch-land, ei - nig Va - ter - land. Al - te Not gilt
Ger - ma - ny, our moth - er - land. Tri - umph o - ver

Adopted in 1950

es zu zwin - gen, und wir zwin - gen sie ver - eint,
by - gone sor - row Can in u - ni - ty be won,
denn es muss uns doch ge - lin - gen, dass die Son - ne schön wie
For we must at - tain a mor - row When o - ver our Ger - ma -
nie ü - ber Deutsch - land scheint, ü - ber Deutsch - land scheint.
ny There is ra - diant sun, there is ra - diant sun.

2 Glück und Friede sei beschieden Deutschland, unsrem
Vaterland. Alle Welt sehnt sich nach Frieden,
reicht den Völkern eure Hand. Wenn wir Brüder-
lich uns einen, schlagen wir des Volkes Feind.
Lasst das Licht des Friedens scheinen, dass nie eine Mutter
mehr ihren Sohn beweint, ihren Sohn beweint!

3 Lasst uns pflügen, lasst uns bauen, lernt und schafft wie
nie zuvor, und der eignen Kraft vertrauend
steigt einfrei Geschlect empor. Deutsche jugend
bestes Streben unsres Volks in dir vereint,
wirst du Deutschlands neues Leben, und die Sonne schön wie
nie über Deutschland scheint, über Deutschland scheint.

English Translation

2 May both joy and peace inspire
Germany, our motherland
Peace is all the world's desire.
To the peoples give your hand.
In fraternity united
We shall crush the people's foe.
May our path by peace be lighted
That no mother shall again
Mourn her son in woe.

3 Let us till and build our nation,
Learn and work as never yet
That a free new generation
Faith in its own strength beget
German youth, for whom the striving
Of our people is at one,
You are Germany's reviving
And over our Germany
There is radiant sun.

GERMANY (WEST)
German Federal Republic

Words by
HEINRICH HOFFMAN VON FALLERSLEBEN (1798-1874)

Music by
FRANZ JOSEPH HAYDN (1732-1809)

Maestoso
Ein - ig - keit und Recht und Frei - heit für das
deut - sche Va - ter - land! Da - nach lasst uns al - le
stre - ben brü - der - lich mit Herz und Hand! Ein - ig -

Authorized as Germany's National Anthem on 11 August, 1922 when the first verse of Heinrich von Fallersleben's poem was sung. In 1950 the Federal Republic adopted the third verse instead as the official words.

Free Translation

Unity and right and freedom
for the German fatherland;
let us all pursue this purpose
brotherly, with heart and hands.
Unity and right and freedom
are the pawns of happiness.
Bis { Flourish in this blessing's glory
flourish, German fatherland

GHANA

Music by
PHILIP GBEHO

Officially became the National Anthem in 1957, the year when independence was attained. The original words were written in 1956, as was the music, but replaced by the present text following a change of government in 1966.

cher - ish fear - less hon - es - ty, And
night or day, in mist or storm, In
help us to re - sist op - pres - sor's rule With all our
ev - 'ry need, what - e'er the call may be, To serve thee,
will and might for ev - er - more. And more.
Gha - na, now and ev - er - more. In more.
1
2
D.C.

3. Raise high the flag of Ghana
And one with Africa advance;
Black Star of hope and honour
To all who thirst for Liberty;
Where the banner of Ghana freely flies,
May the way to freedom truly lie;
Arise, arise, O sons of Ghanaland,
And under God march on for evermore!

GREAT BRITAIN

God Save The Queen

Origin of both words and melody obscure.
Earliest copy of words in Gentleman's Magazine, 1745.

2. O Lord our God arise,
Scatter her enemies,
And make them fall:
Confound their politics,
Frustrate their knavish tricks,
On Thee our hopes we fix:
God save us all.

3. Thy choicest gifts in store,
On her be pleased to pour;
Long may she reign:
May she defend our laws,
And ever give us cause
To sing with heart and voice
God save the Queen.

GREECE

Words by
DIONYSIOS SOLOMÓS (1798-1857)
English versification by
T.M. CARTLEDGE

Music by
NIKOLAOS MANTZAROS (1795-1873)

Maestoso
p
Seg - no - rees a - po tin kop - si too spath-
I shall al - ways re - cog - nise you By the
p
f
-yoo tin tro - me - ri; Seg - no - rees a - po tin
dread - ful sword you hold, As the earth, with search - ing
f
p
op - si poo me vya me - tra tin yee. Ap ta
vis - ion, You sur - vey, with spi - rit bold. 'Twas the

Chosen as National Anthem of Greece by King George I and adopted in 1864.
Of the 158 verses, the first two which are given are those usually sung.

kok - ka-la vyal-me - nee ton el-lee - non ta ye
Greeks of old whose dy - ing Brought to birth our spi - rit
f
ra Ke san prawt' an - three - o -
free. Now, with an - cient val - our
f
ff
-me - nee hye - r'o hye - ri e-lef - the-rya. Ke san
ris - ing, Let us hail you, oh Li - ber-ty! Now, with
ff

prawt' an - three - o - me - nee hye - r'o hye r'e - lef - the -
an - cient val - our ris - ing, Let us hail you, Li - ber -
-rya, Ke san prawt' an - three - o -
-ty, Now, with an - cient val - our
-me - nee hye - r'o hye - r'e - lef - the - rya.
ris - ing, Let us hail you, Li - ber - ty!

GREENLAND

nangminekκ erinalik

Words by
HENRIK LUND (1875-1948)

Music by
JONATHAN PETERSEN (1881-1961)
Arr. by HENRY COLEMAN

2. *akugdleκutaussutut merdlertutut*
ilingne perortugut tamâne
kalâtdlinik ingminik taiumavugut
niarκuvit atarκinartup sâne!

3. *atortitdlugitdlo tamaisa pisit*
ingerdlaniarusuleκaugut
nutarterdlugitdlo noκitsigissatit
sujumut, sujumut piumaκaugut

This is Greenland's National Song. The Danish National Anthem is also used.

4. *inersimalersut ingerdlanerat*
tungâlítiterusulekárput
okautsit »avîsit« kanok kinguneʀat
atúsassok erinigilekárput.

5. *takigdlune nâme atúngivekaok,*
kâlâtdlit, sujumut makigitse!
inugtut inûnek pigiuminakaok
saperase isumakaleritse!

Free Translation

1. Our immemorial land under the beacon of gleaming ice
With glowing snow hair around your head!
You faithful mother, who carried us in your embrace,
While ocean game of your coasts you promised us.

2. As immature children we have sprung from your soil
And grown up with you among your mountains .
Our name is Kalatdlit, in the deep track of legend
Venerated for the age of its white countenance.

3. And all the while your wealth was used for our good,
We longed for the new forms of the world :
Released from the tight bands in the homeland circle
Now advance ; forward towards distant objects we rush.

4. You grown-up nations, stretch out your hand !
Your track we long soon to follow .
A world of books shall urge forward the spirit
Which carries us up on the wave of new learning.

5. Impossible now to tarry inactive longer
Kalatdlit, stand up! Meet the new day !
As free-born beings from now on we will grow,
Begin to have faith in the dawn of ability!

GRENADA

Words by
IRVA BAPTISTE

Music by
LOUIS MASANTO, Jr.

Maestoso
Hail! Gre-na - da, land of ours, We pledge our-selves to thee, Heads,
hearts and hands in u - ni-ty To reach our des - ti - ny. Ev-er

Grenada became independent 7 February 1974

con - scious of God, Be-ing proud of our her - it - age, May
we with faith and cour-age As - pire,— build, ad - vance As one
peo - ple, one fam - i-ly. God bless our na - tion.

GUATEMALA

Words by
JOSÉ JOAQUÍN PALMA (1844-1911)
Translated by
JOSÉ P. UGARTE
Versified by
MARTIN, MARY ELIZABETH and DICCON SHAW

Music by
RAFAEL ÁLVAREZ (b.1858)

This was chosen from entries in a public competition in 1887

Adopted by governmental decree of 28 October, 1896 and 19 February, 1897, and modified by decree of 26 July, 1934

VERSE
p
¡Gua - te - ma - la fe - liz! que tus a - ras no pro -
Gua - te - ma - la, blest land, home of hap - py race, May thine
p
f rall.
a tempo
-fa - ne ja - más el ver - du - go; ni ha-ya es - cla - vos que la - man el
al - tars pro - fa - ned be nev - er; No yoke of sla - ver - y weigh on thee
f
rall.
a tempo
yu - go ni ti - ra - nos que es-cu - pan tu faz. Si ma -
e - ver, Nor may ty - rants e'er spit in thy face. Should to -

-ña - na tu sue - lo sa - gra - do lo a-me - na-za in-va-sión ex-tran -
-mor - row see me-naced thy sa - cred soil By in - va - ders all pi - ty de -

frall.
a tempo
-je - ra, li - bre al vien - to tu her - mo - sa ban -
-ny - ing, Your loved flag to the winds free - ly
frall.
a tempo

-de - ra a ven - cer o a mo - rir lla - ma - rá.
fly - ing Will call you to con - quer or die.

CHORUS
Li-bre al vien - to tu her-mo - sa ban - de - ra a ven -
Your loved flag to the winds free-ly fly - ing Will
f
-cer o a mo-rir lla-ma - rá; que tu pue-blo con á - ni - ma
call you to con-quer or die. You would soon-er be slain fight-ing
f
fie - ra an-tes muer - to q'es - cla - vo se - rá.
brave - ly Than sub - ject - ed in sla - ve-ry lie.

GUINEA

Liberté

No words

Music by
ALFA YAYA
Arr. by KEITA FODÉBA
and J. CELLIER

Became independent 2 October 1958

GUINEA – BISSAU

Words and Music by
AMILCAR CABRAL (1924 - 1973)

Allegro moderato, alla marcia

f

mf
1. Sol, su - or e o ver - de e mar, Se - cu - los de dor e es-peran-ça:
2. Ra - mos do mes - mo tron - co, Ol - los na mes-ma luz:
3

Es - ta é a ter - ra dos nos - sos a - vós! Fru - to das nos - sas mãos,
Es - ta é a for - ça da nos - sa u-nião! Can - tem o mar e a ter - ra
3

Composed in 1963.

Adopted as the National Anthem on Independence Day, 24th September 1974.

cresc.
Da flôr do nos - so san - gue: Es - ta é a nos - sa pá - tria a
A ma - dru - ga - da eo sol Que a nos - sa lu - ta fe - cun -
cresc.
f p mf
ma - da.
dou!
Vi - va a pá - tri - a glo - ri - o - sa! Flo -
f p mf
riu nos céus A ban - dei - ra lu - ta. A - van - te, con - tra o
cresc.
ju - go es - tran - gei - ro! Nós va - mos con - stru - ir Na
cresc.

Verse 1 Sun, sweat, verdure and sea,
Centuries of pain and hope;
This is the land of our ancestors.
Fruit of our hands,
Of the flower of our blood:
This is our beloved country.

Verse 2 Branches of the same trunk,
Eyes in the same light;
This is the force of our unity!
The sea and the land,
The dawn and the sun are singing
That our struggle has borne fruit!

Chorus Long live our glorious country!
The banner of our struggle
Has fluttered in the skies.
Forward, against the foreign yoke!
We are going to build
Peace and progress
In our immortal country!

GUYANA

Words by
A. L. LUKER (1917-1971)

Music by
R. C. G. POTTER

mf
1. Dear land of Guy - a - na, of ri - vers and
2. Green land of Guy - a - na, our he - roes of
mf
plains, Made rich by the sun - shine and
yore, Both bonds - - men and free, laid their
lush by the rains, Set gem - - like and
bones on your shore; This soil so they

The words and music were selected as the result of a competition. This anthem was approved by the House of Assembly on 21st April, 1966. Guyana became independent 26th May, 1966.

fair ___ be-tween moun - tains and sea, ___ Your
hal - lowed, and from them ___ are we, ___ All

child - ren sa - lute you, dear land ___ of the free.
sons of one mo - ther, Guy - a - - na the free.

3. Great land of Guyana, diverse though our strains,
We are born of their sacrifice, heirs of their pains,
And ours is the glory their eyes did not see -
One land of six peoples, united and free.

4. Dear land of Guyana, to you will we give
Our homage, our service, each day that we live;
God guard you, great Mother, and make us to be
More worthy our heritage - land of the free.

HAITI

La Dessalinienne

Words by
JUSTIN LHÉRISSON (1873-1907)
English versification by
MARTIN SHAW
(First verse by
DICCON SHAW and MARY ELIZABETH SHAW)

Music by
NICOLAS GEFFRARD
(1871-1930)

Alla marcia
f
1. Pour le Pa-ys Pour les An - cê - tres, Marchons u -
1. March on! for an - ces-tors and coun - try, U - ni - ted
f

nis, mar-chons u - nis Dans nos rangs point de
march, U - ni - ted march; Lo - yal sub - jects all re -

traî - tres! Du sol soy-ons seuls maî - tres. Mar -
- main, And lords of our do - main. U -
ff
ff

This anthem was composed for the centenary of national independence in 1904. The title is derived from Jean-Jacques Dessalines, the founder of Haiti as an independent republic, of which he crowned himself Emperor.

-chons u-nis, mar - chons u-nis Pour le Pa -
-ni - ted march, march on! U-ni - ted march for
-ys, pour les An - cê - tres Mar - chons marchons mar -
an - ces - tors and coun - try, March on, u-ni - ted
-chons u - nis Pour le Pa - ys, pour les An - cê - tres!
march, march on! U-nite for an - ces - tors and coun - try!

2. *Pour les Aieux*
Pour la Patrie
Bêchons joyeux:
Quand le champ fructifie
L'âme se fortifie
Bêchons joyeux
Pour les Aïeux,
Pour la Patrie.

3. *Pour le Pays*
Et pour nos Pères
Formons des Fils.
Libres, forts et prospères,
Toujours: nous serons frères,
Formons des fils
Pour le Pays
Et pour nos Pères.

4. *Pour les Aïeux*
Pour la Patrie
O Dieu des Preux!
Sous ta garde infinie
Prends nos droits, notre vie,
O Dieu des Preux!
Pour les Aïeux,
Pour la Patrie.

5. *Pour le Drapeau*
Pour la Patrie,
Mourir est beau!
Notre passé nous crie:
Ayez l'âme aguerrie!
Mourir est beau
Pour le Drapeau,
Pour la Patrie.

2. For sacred soil,
For sires of old
We gladly toil.
When teem field and wold
The soul is strong and bold.
We gladly toil, we gladly toil
For sacred soil,
For sires of old.

3. For land we love
And sires of old
We give our sons.
Free, happy, and bold,
One brotherhood we'll hold.
We give our sons, we give our sons
For land we love
And sires of old.

4. For those who gave
For country all,
God of the brave,
To thee, O God, we call;
Without thee we must fall,
God of the brave, God of the brave.
For those who gave
For country all.

5. For flag on high
For Native land
'Tis fine to die.
Our traditions demand
Be ready, heart and hand,
'Tis fine to die, 'tis fine to die
For flag on high,
For Native land.

HONDURAS

Words by
AUGUSTO C. COELLO (1881-1941)
English versification by
J. E. HALES
(From the translation by
Señor TIBURCIO CARIAS h,)

Music by
CARLOS HARTLING
(1875-1919)

Tempo di Marcia
con energia
ff CHORUS
Tu ban-de - ra, tu ban-de - - ra es un
As your stan - dard, as your stan - - dard serves a
ff

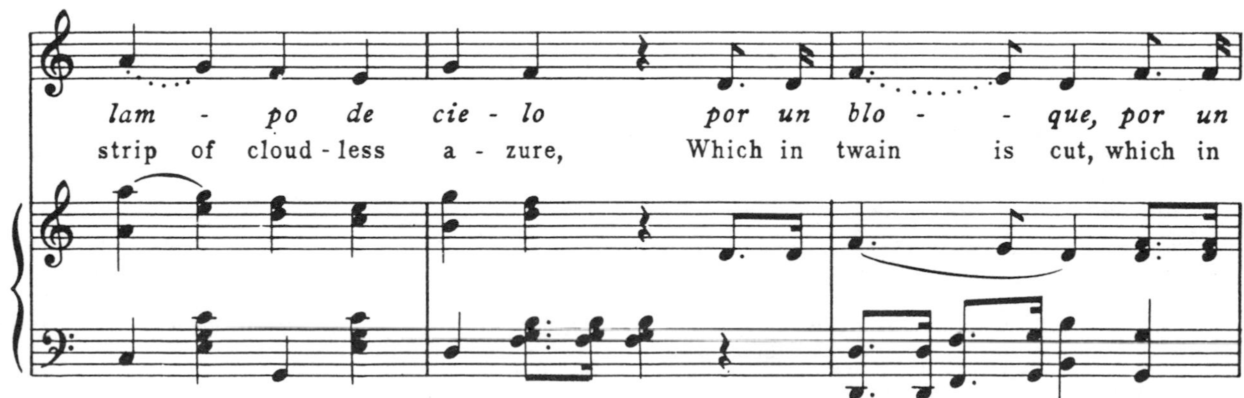
lam - po de cie - lo por un blo - - que, por un
strip of cloud-less a - zure, Which in twain is cut, which in

blo - - que de_ nie - ve cru - za - do; y se
twain is cut by a band that snows be - sprin - kle; In whose
mp
mp

This anthem was selected as result of a public competition. It was adopted as the National Anthem in 1915.

ven en su fon - do sa - gra - do cin - co es -
sa - cred ab - yss - es there twin - kle Five pale
- tre - llas de pá - li - do a - zul; en tu em -
stars lit with soft - est rays of blue. And in your
- ble - ma que un mar ru - mo - ro - so con sus
shield, that a stri - dent sea is guard - ing With the
on - das bra - ví - as es - cu - da, De un vol -
bul - wark of its sav - age bil - lows' might, A vol -
ff
ff

-cán, de un vol-cán tras la
ca - - no stands, a vol-ca - - no stands, from whose
ci - ma des - nu - da hay un as - tro, hay un
lone-ly sum-mit's height Comes the bea - con clear, comes the
as - - tro de ni - ti - da luz.
bea - con clear, of a star that flash-es there.
Fine
Meno mosso
p VERSE
In - dia, vir - gen y her-mo - sa dor-mi - as de tus
In - dia, like a fair maid you were sleep - ing To the
p
Ped.
Ped.
sim.

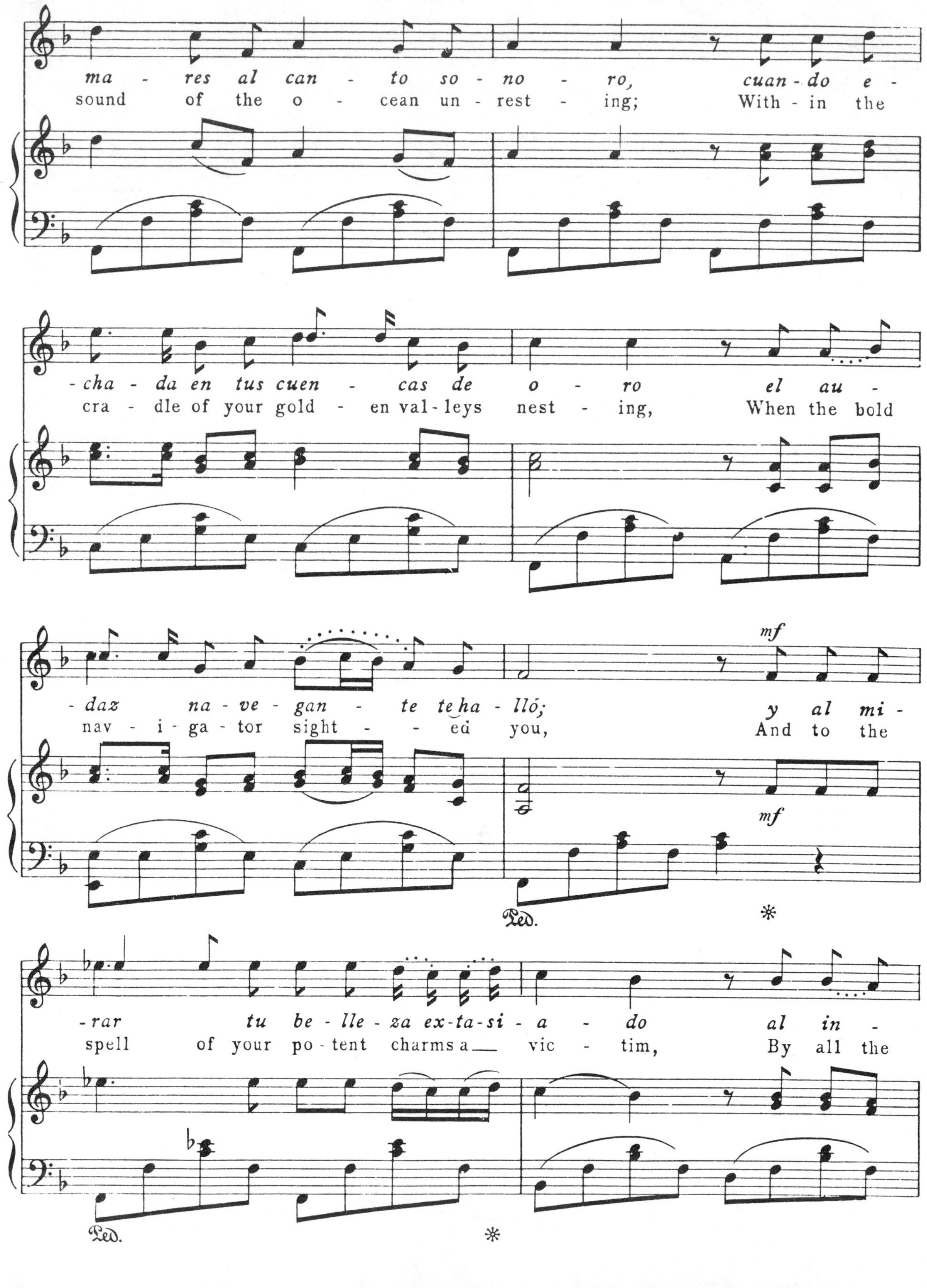

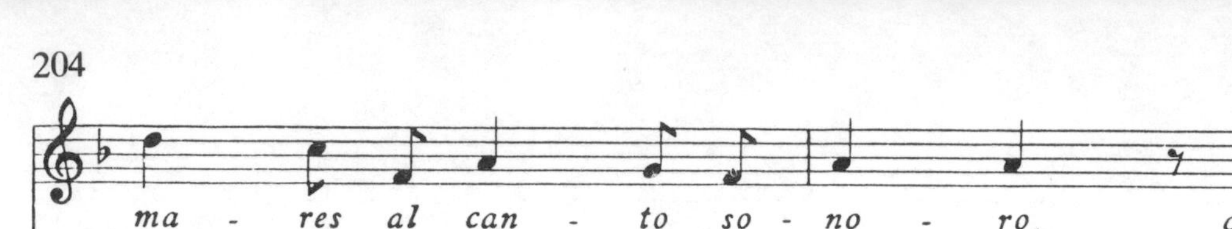

ma - res al can - to so - no - ro, cuan - do e -
sound of the o - cean un - rest - ing; With - in the
-cha - da en tus cuen - cas de o - ro el au -
cra - dle of your gold - en val - leys nest - ing, When the bold
-daz na - ve - gan - te te ha - lló; y al mi -
nav - i - ga - tor sight - ed you, And to the
mf
mf
Ped.
-rar tu be - lle - za ex - ta - si - a - do al in -
spell of your po - tent charms a vic - tim, By all the
Ped.

ff
-flu - jo i-de-al de tu en - can - to, la
mar - vels of your love - li - ness en - chant - ed, De -
ff
or - la a - zul de tu es-plén - di - do
-vout - ly a kiss love - la - den he im -
Ped. Ped. Ped. Ped.
man - to con su be - so de a-mor con-sa - gró.
-plant - ed On your man - tle's rich mar - gin of blue.
Ped. * Ped. *
D.C. al Fine

Last Verse

Por guardar ese emblema divino,
marcharemos Oh Patria a la muerte,
generosa será nuestra suerte,
si morimos pensando en tu amor.—
Defendiendo tu santa bandera
y en tus pliegues gloriosos cubiertos,
serán muchos, Oh Honduras tus muertos,
pero todos caerán con honor.—

In defence of our glorious emblem
We are ready, my Country, to perish,
For future ages their fame will ever cherish
Who in their dying hour are thinking of your love.
In the defence of your holy banner fallen,
Their lifeless forms in its hallowed folds enshrouded.
Not few, blessed Honduras, shall be your proud dead,
But they all in honour's cause will die.

HUNGARY

Words by
FERENC KÖLCSEY (1790-1838)

Music by
FERENC ERKEL (1810-1893)
Arr. by HENRY COLEMAN

Andante maestoso
mf
Ped.
poco rit.
dim.
p
a tempo
p
Is - ten áldd meg a ma - gyart Jó kedv - vel bő -
God bless the Hun - gar - i - ans Give them joy and
- ség - gel. Nyújts fe - lè - je vé - dő kart,
plen - ty Pro - tect their bat - tal - i - ons

Ferenc Erkel was the creator of the Hungarian romantic Grand Opera. From 1875-1886 he was Director of the National Academy of Music, and he founded in 1867 the National Association of Hungarian Choirs.

This was awarded first prize in a national competition in 1844 when it was officially adopted.

mf
Ha küzd el - len - ség - gel. Bal - sors a - kit
When they fight the en - e - my. Lift their sor - rows
mf
cresc.
ré - gen tép Hozz re - a vig esz - ten - döt.
and their tears, Bring them hap - py pros-perous years.
cresc.
f
Meg - bün-höd - te már e nép A múl - tat sjö - ven -
All its past and fut - ure sins This peo - ple has a -
f
döt.
- toned.
mf
p

ICELAND

Lofsöngur

Words by
MATTHIAS JOCHUMSSON (1835-1920)

Music by
SVEINBJÖRN SVEINBJÖRNSSON
(1847-1927)

Written and composed in 1874, when Iceland secured its own constitution and also celebrated the one thousandth anniversary of the first permanent settlers of Europeans (Norwegians) on the island.

Free Translation

Our country's God! Our country's God!
We worship Thy name in its wonder sublime
The suns of the heavens are set in Thy crown
By Thy legions, the ages of time!
With Thee is each day as a thousand years,
Each thousand of years, but a day.
Eternity's flow'r with its homage of tears,
That reverently passes away.
  Iceland's thousand years!
Eternity's flow'r, with its homage of tears,
That reverently passes away.

INDIA

Jană Gană Mană

Words and melody by
RABINDRANATH TAGORE (1861-1941)
Arr. by BRYSON GERRARD

Officially adopted by the Indian Constitutional Assembly on 24th January 1950, two days before the proclamation of the Republic.

First published 1912, it was for some years prior to adoption associated with India's struggle for independence.

Ya - mu-nă, Gan - gā, Uch' ha-lă ja - la-dhī ta ran - gă.

Ta-va shu-bhă nā - mé jā - gé, Ta-va shu-bhă ā - shī - shă

mā - gé, gā-ve ta-vă ja - yă gā - thā. Ja-nă ga-nă man - ga-lă

dā ya-kă ja-yă hé Bhā - ra-tă bhā - gyă vi - dhā - tā. Ja-yă

*See Footnote 2

mp

pu - ra - bă pas - hchi - mă ā - té té ré sim - ha sa - nă

mp

pā - să pré - mă - hā — ră ko gu - thé.

8ves

Ja - nă ga - nă ai kyă vi - dhā - ya - kă ja - yă hé! Bhā - ra - tă bhā - gyă vi -

8ves

f

dhā - tā. Ja - yă hé! Ja - yă hé! Ja - yă hé!

f

8ves

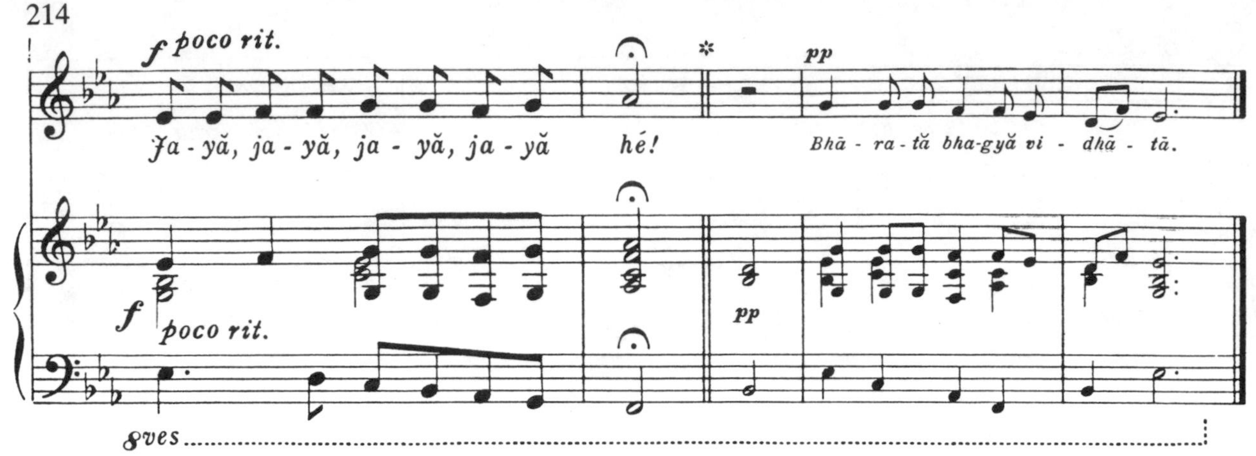

Free Translation

Thou art the ruler of the minds
of all people,
Thou Dispenser of India's destiny,
Thy name rouses the hearts
of the Punjab, Sind,
Gujrat and Maratha, of Dravid,
Orissa and Bengal.
It echoes in the hills of
the Vindhyas and Himalayas,
Mingles in the music of
Jumna and Ganges,
and is chanted by the waves
of the Indian sea.
They pray for thy blessing
and sing thy praise,
Thou Dispenser of India's destiny,
Victory, Victory, Victory to thee!

* *Note 1.* It will be noticed that the tune ends on the subdominant. The two bars in small notes at the end are not infrequently added — but they are not part of the original melody.

2. For ordinary performances it is usual to end at the first asterisk.

3. The Bengali words of the song have been transliterated for English readers and should therefore be pronounced as in English, i.e. 'J' as in the English 'John'. 'Hs' should be lightly aspirated, even in 'th' which is pronounced as in 'at home' said rather quickly. 'Sh' and 'ch', however, remain as in English; 'g' is always hard; 'é' as in French.

INDONESIA

Indonesia Raya

Words and Music by
WAGE RUDOLF SUPRATMAN
(1903-1938)

Maestoso
f
f
1. In - do - ne - sia ___ ta - nah a - - ir - ku Ta - nah tum - pah da - rah - ku. Di - sa -
2. In - do - ne - sia! ___ Ta - nah jang mu - lia, Ta - nah ki - ta jang ka - ja. Di - sa -
3. In - do - ne - sia! ___ Ta - nah jang su - tji, Ta - nah ki - ta jang sak - ti. Di - sa -

This was adopted as the Nationalist Party Song in 1928, and became the National Anthem in 1949.

-na - lah___ a-ku ber - di - ri Dja - di pan - du i - bu -
-na - lah___ a-ku ber - a - da Un - tuk s'la - ma - la - ma -
-na - lah___ a-ku ber - di - ri 'Ndja - ga i - bu se - dja -
-ku. In - do - ne - sia___ ke-bang-sa-an - ku, Bang - sa
-nja. In - do - ne - sia___ Ta-nah pu - sa - ka, P'sa - ka
-ti. In - do - ne - sia___ Ta-nah ber - se - ri, Ta - nah
dan Ta - nah A - ir - ku. Ma - ri - lah ki - ta ber -
Ki - ta se - mu - a - nja. Ma - ri - lah ki - ta men -
jang a - ku sa - ja - ngi. Ma - ri - lah ki - ta ber -
-se - ru "In - do - ne - sia ber - sa - tu." Hi - dup -
-do - 'a, "In - do - ne - sia ba - ha - gia!" Su - bur -
-djan - dji, "In - do - ne - sia a - ba - di!" S'la - mat -
mf
mf

-lah ta - nah - ku, Hi - dup - lah ne - gri - ku, Bang - sa-
-lah Ta - nah - nja, Su - bur - lah dji - wa - nja, Bang - sa-
-lah Rak - jat - nja, S'la - mat - lah pu - tra - nja, Pu - lau-
-ku, Rak - jat - ku se - 'm - wa - - nja. Ba - ngun-
-nja, Rak - jat - nja se - 'm - wa - - nja. Sa - dar-
-nja, la - ut - nja se - 'm - wa - - nja. Ma - dju-
-lah dji - wa - nja, Ba - ngun - lah ba - dan - nja Un - tuk
-lah ha - ti - nja, Sa - dar - lah bu - di - nja Un - tuk
-lah Ne - gri - nja, Ma - dju - lah Pan - du - nja Un - tuk
In - do - ne - sia Ra - ja.
In - do - ne - sia Ra - ja. In - do-
In - do - ne - sia Ra - ja.
ff
ff

-ne - sia Ra-ja, Mer - de-ka, Mer - de-ka, Ta - nah-
-ku ne - gri - ku jang ku - tjin - - ta. In - do-
-ne - sia Ra - ja, Mer - de - ka, Mer - de-ka, Hi - dup-
molto ritard. 2nd time
-lah In - do - ne - sia Ra - ja. In - do- - ja.
1
2
molto ritard. 2nd time

Free Translation

1 INDONESIA, our native country
Consecrated with our spilt blood
Where we all arise to stand guard
Over this our Motherland:
Indonesia our nationality
Our people and our country.
Come then, let us all demand
Indonesia united.
Long live our land
Long live our state
Our nation, our people, and all
Arouse then its spirit,
Organise its own bodies
To obtain Indonesia the Great.

2 INDONESIA, an eminent country,
Our wealthy country
There we shall be forever.
Indonesia, the country of our
ancestors,
A relic of all of us.
Let us pray
For Indonesia's prosperity:
May her soil be fertile
And spirited her soul,
The nation and all the people.
Conscious be her heart
And her mind
For Indonesia the Great.

3 INDONESIA, a sacred country,
Our victorious country:
There we stand
Guarding our true Mother.
Indonesia, a beaming Country,
A country we love with all our heart,
Let's make a vow
That Indonesia be there forever.
Blessed be her people
And her sons,
All her islands, and her seas.
Fast be the country's progress
And the progress of her youth
For Indonesia the Great.

CHORUS INDONESIA the Great, independent and free,
My beloved land and country.
Indonesia the Great, independent and free,
Long live Indonesia the Great.

IRAN

Imperial Salute

Words by
M. H. AFSAR (1880-1940)
English versification by
FRANCIS GOULDING and T. M. CARTLEDGE
from a translation by MAS'UUD FARZAAD

Music by
DAVOOD NAJMI MOGHADDAM
(b? 1900)

Allegro moderato
1. Shah - han - sha - he - maw zen - de baw daw
1. Long live the Shah, our King of Kings, And
Paw - yad kesh - var - be - far - rash jaw - ve - dawn. Kez
may his glo - ry make im - mor - tal our land. For
Pah - le - vee shood mulk - e I - rawn Sad - rah beh - tar ze - e
Pah - le - vi im - proved I - ran A hun - dred - fold from where it

Adopted in 1933.

p
'uhde baw - se - tan. Az dush-man-awn boo - dee par-eesh awn
once used to stand. Though once be - set by the foe-men's rage,
p
Dar saw - ye - yash aw - soo - de I - rawn. I - ran - i - awn
Now it has peace in his keep-ing sure; We of I - ran, re -
f
pay - vas - te shaw dawn Ham - var - e yaz dawn Bu - vad oo - ra ne - gah - bawn.
- joice in ev - 'ry age. Oh, may God pro - tect him both now and ev - er - more.
f

2. *Ay! Par-chamm-i-khoor-sheed-i-I-rawn*
Par-to af-kann be roo-yi-een Je-hawn
Yawd aw-varr az oon roo-ze-gaw-ree
Kaw-sood az bar-qi-tee-ghat harr ke-rawn.
Dan saw-yè-yat jawn-mee-fa-shaw-neem
Az dush-man-awn jawn mee-se-taw-neem
Maw vaw-ress-i-mul-ki-kay-aw-neem
Ham-ee-shè khaw-heem vat-tan-naw az del-lo-jawn.

3. *Boo-dee-mo has-teem pai-ru-vi-haqq.*
Juz haqq harr-gez na-khaw-heem az Je-hawn
Baw shah-pa-ras-tee mam-li-kat-raw
Daw-reem az dass-ti-dush-man darr em-awn.
Maw pai-ru-vi ker-dawr-i-neek-eem
Ro-shan-dell az pan-daw-ri-neek-eem
Rakh-shan-dè az goof-taw-ri-neek-eem
Shoo-dzeen faz-zaw-'el bu-lan-daw vaw-zè I-rawn.

2. Oh, Sun that shines on Iran's banner,
Shed upon each nation rays strong and fair.
Those days keep in our recollection
When thy flashing sword brought peace everywhere.
We give our lives in thy shade benign,
And take the lives of each enemy.
We are the heirs of Kianis' line;
Oh, belovèd land, ever wholly thine are we.

3. Of Right we've been and still are champions.
What is right is all we ever demand.
Through worship of the King, we ever
From the enemy will guard this our land.
"Good Deeds" the first virtue of our call,
"Good Thoughts" the light our hearts and minds to guide,
And through "Good Speech" shining, one and all,
This is Iran's fame that will echo far and wide.

IRAQ

No words

Music by
L. ZAMBAKA

This became the National Anthem in 1959, when it was composed.

IRISH REPUBLIC

Amhrán na bhFiann

THE SOLDIER'S SONG

Words by
PEADAR KEARNEY (1883-1942)

Music by
PEADAR KEARNEY and PATRICK HEANEY
Arr. by T. M. CARTLEDGE

By permission of Minister of Finance, Éire.
Chorus adopted as Irish National Anthem, July 1926

fonn - mhar faobh - rach — sinn chun gleo, 'S go tiúr - mhar glé roimh
- pa - tient for — the — com - ing fight, And as we wait the
cresc.
f
thiocht do'n ló, Fé chiú - nas — chaomh na hoi - che ar — seol: Seo libh,
morn - ing's light, — Here in the si - lence of — the — night, We'll
cresc.
f
CHORUS
can-aidh Amh-rán na bhFiann. Sinn - ne Fian - na Fáil A -
chant a sol - dier's song. Sol - diers are we, Whose
- tá fé gheall ag Éir - inn, Buidhean dár sluagh Thar
lives are pledged to Ire - land; Some have come From a

tuinn do ráin - ig chúghainn, Fé — mhóid bheith saor. Sean-
land be-yond the wave. Sworn — to be free, No
- tír ár sinn - sear feas - ta Ní fág - far fé'n tío - rán ná fé'n
more our an - cient sire - land Shall shel - ter the des - pot or the
tráil. A - nocht a thé - am sa — bheár - na bhaoghail, Le
slave. To - night we man — the — bear - na baoghail In
gean ar Ghaedhil chun báis nó saoghail, Le gun - a - sgréach, fé
Er - in's cause, come woe or weal; 'Mid can - nons' roar and
p
cresc.
f

ff
rit.
D.C.
lámhach na — bpiléar, Seo libh, can-aidh Amh-rán na bhFiann.
ri - fles'— peal We'll chant a sol - dier's song.
D.C.
ff
rit.

2. *Cois bánta réidhe, ar árdaibh sléibhe,*
Ba bhuadhach ár sinnsear romhainn,
Ag lámhach go tréan fé'n sár-bhrat séin
Tá thuas sa ghaoith go seolta.
Ba dhúthchas riamh d'ár gcine cháidh
Gan iompáil siar ó imirt áir,
'S ag siubhal mar iad i gcoinnibh námhad
Seo libh, canaidh Amhrán na bhFiann.

CURFÁ: Sinn-ne Fianna Fáil, etc.

3. *A bhuidhean nách fann d'fhuil Ghaoidheal is Gall,*
Sin breacadh lae na saoirse,
Tá sgeimhle 's sgannradh i gcroidhthibh namhad,
Roimh ranngaibh laochra ár dtíre.
Ár dteinte is tréith gan spréach anois,
Sin luisne ghlé san spéir anoir,
'S an bíodhbha i raon na bpiléar agaibh:
Seo libh, canaidh Amhrán na bhFiann.

CURFÁ: Sinn-ne Fianna Fáil, etc.

2. In valley green, on towering crag,
Our fathers fought before us,
And conquered 'neath the same old flag
That's proudly floating o'er us.
We're children of a fighting race,
That never yet has known disgrace,
And as we march, the foe to face,
We'll chant a soldier's song.

CHORUS: Soldiers are we, etc.

3. Sons of the Gael! Men of the Pale!
The long watched day is breaking;
The serried ranks of Inisfail
Shall set the Tyrant quaking.
Our camp fires now are burning low:
See in the east a silv'ry glow,
Out yonder waits the Saxon foe,
So chant a soldier's song.

CHORUS: Soldiers are we, etc.

ISLE OF MAN

Arrane Ashoonagh Dy Vannin

Words by
WILLIAM HENRY GILL
(1839-1922)
Manx translation by
JOHN J. KNEEN
(1873-1939)

Music adapted by
WILLIAM HENRY GILL
(1839-1922)
from a Traditional Manx Air

The main National Anthem is that for Great Britain. This anthem was dedicated to The Lady Raglan, 1907. There are 8 verses in all.

W.H.Gill, a keen Manxman, was a collector and arranger of Manx music, of which he made a special study. J.J. Kneen was an expert on the Manx language and author of several books on it. For his scholarship he was awarded the Order of St Olaf by H.M. The King of Norway, in recognition also of the historical connection between Norway and the Isle of Man.

ISRAEL

Hatikvah

THE HOPE

Words by
NAFTALI HERZ IMBER
(1856-1909)

Melody traditional

Maestoso
p
Kol_ od ba-le - vav pe - ni - mah Ne - fesh ye-hu - di
p
ho - mi-yah, Ul-fa-a-tei_miz-rach ka - di - mah A - yin le-zi - on
mp
mp
zo - fi - yah. Od lo av - dah tik-va-te - nu Ha - tik - vah bat
f
f
ff
ff

Hatikva is now firmly established as the Anthem of the State of Israèl as well as the Jewish National Anthem

Free Translation

While yet within the heart-inwardly
The soul of the Jew yearns,
And towards the vistas of the East-eastwards
An eye to Zion looks.
'Tis not yet lost, our hope,
The hope of two thousand years,
To be a free people in our land
In the land of Zion and Jerusalem.

ITALY

Inno di Mameli

Words by
GOFFREDO MAMELI
(1827-1849)

Music by
MICHELE NOVARO
(1822-1885)

Adopted as National Anthem 2nd June, 1946, on the establishment of the Italian Republic.

-tel - li d'I - ta - lia, l'I - ta - lia s'è
de - sta, del - l'el - mo di Sci - pio s'è
cin - ta la te - sta. Do - v'è la vit -
-to - ria? Le por - ga la chio - ma, chè schia - va di
rall.
a tempo
f
f a tempo
rall.

Ro - ma Id - di - o la ___ cre - ò.
ff
pp
pp
Fratel - li d'I - ta - lia, l'I - ta - lia s'è
de - sta, dell'el - mo di Sci - pio s'è cin - ta la te - sta. Dov'è la vit-
cresc.
cresc.
- to - ria? Le por - ga la chio - ma, che schia - va di Ro - ma Iddio la cre-
f
f

Free Translation

Italian Brothers,
Italy has arisen,
Has put on the helmet of Scipio.
Where is Victory?
Created by God
The slave of Rome,
She crowns you with glory.
Let us unite,
We are ready to die,
Italy calls.

IVORY COAST

l'Abidjanaise

Words by MATHIEU EKRA
in collaboration with JOACHIM BONY
and the Abbé COTY

Music by the Abbé
PIERRE MICHEL PANGO
Arr. by HENRY COLEMAN

This National Anthem was adopted at the declaration of independence on 7th August, 1960
The music was composed by an Ivory Coast priest.
Mathieu Ekra is Minister of Information and Joachim Bony Minister of Education in the Ivory Coast.

- heur. ___ Fiers I - voi - riens, le pa - ys nous ap -
- pel - le. Si nous a - vons dans la paix ra - me -
- né la li - ber - té, No - tre de - voir se - ra d'être
un mo - dè - le De l'es - pé - ran - ce ___ pro - mise

ff
3
à l'hu-ma-ni-té, En for-geant, u-nie dans la
foi nou-vel-le, la pa-trie de la vraie fra-ter-ni-té.

English Paraphrase by
ELIZABETH P. COLEMAN

We salute you, O land of hope, country of hospitality; thy gallant legions have restored thy dignity.

Belovèd Ivory Coast, thy sons, proud builders of thy greatness, all mustered together for thy glory, in joy will construct thee.

Proud citizens of the Ivory Coast, the country calls us. If we have brought back liberty peacefully, it will be our duty to be an example of the hope promised to humanity, forging unitedly in new faith the Fatherland of true brotherhood.

JAMAICA

Words by
The Rev. HUGH SHERLOCK (b.1905)

Music by
ROBERT LIGHTBOURNE
Arr. by MAPLETOFT POULLE

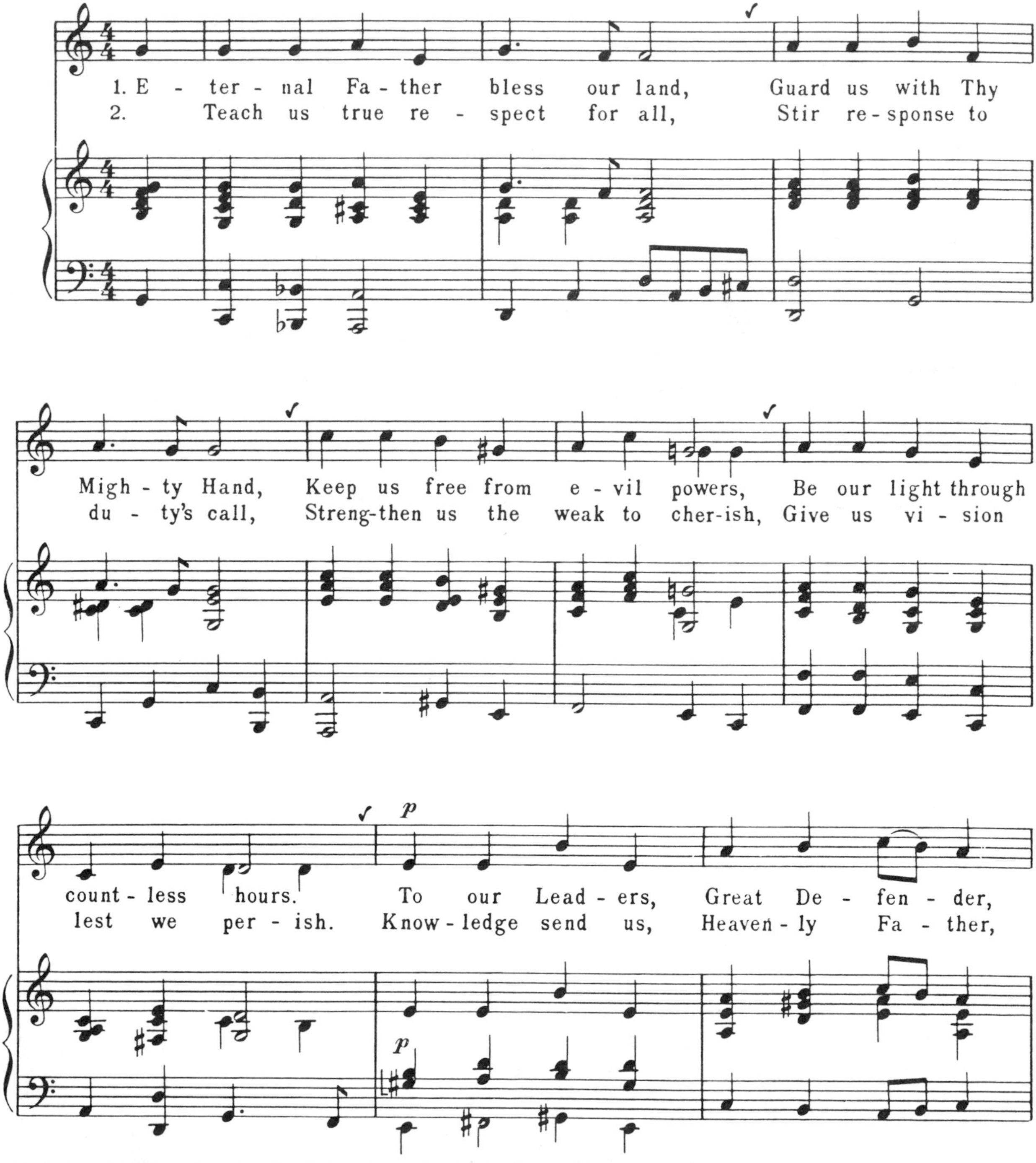

1. E - ter - nal Fa - ther bless our land, Guard us with Thy
2. Teach us true re - spect for all, Stir re - sponse to
Migh - ty Hand, Keep us free from e - vil powers, Be our light through
du - ty's call, Streng-then us the weak to cher-ish, Give us vi - sion
p
count - less hours. To our Lead - ers, Great De - fen - der,
lest we per - ish. Know - ledge send us, Heaven - ly Fa - ther,
p

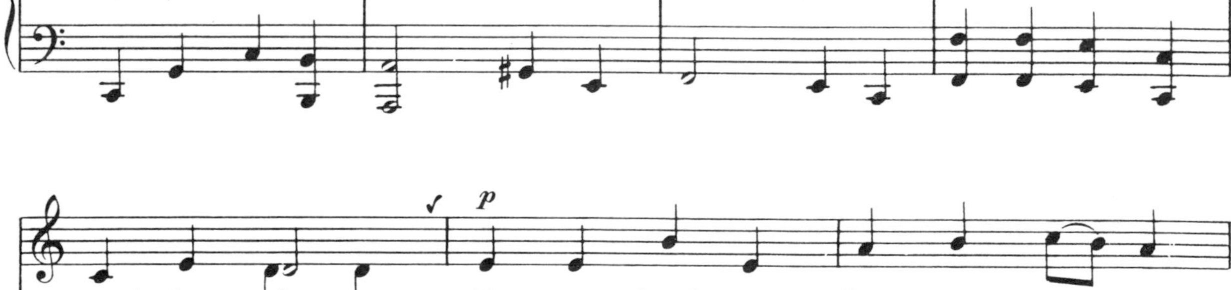

This was officially selected as the National Anthem by the House of Representatives in Jamaica on 19th July 1962. Robert Lightbourne is a Jamaican and Minister of Trade and Industry at the time of composing the Anthem. The Rev. Sherlock, a Jamaican, has for many years been associated with "Boys' Town" in one of the poorer districts of Kingston.

mf
Grant true wis - dom from a - bove. Just - ice, Truth, be
mf
ours for - ev - er, Ja - mai - ca, land we love. Ja-
3
f allargando
ff rall.
- mai - ca, Ja - mai - ca, Ja - mai - ca, land we love.
f allargando
ff rall.

JAPAN

THE PEACEFUL REIGN

Words selected from the seventh volume of *Kokinshu* dating from the 9th century
English translation by
SAKUZO TAKADA

Music composed by court musicians and selected in 1880 by
HIROMORI HAYASHI

♩= 69
p
mf
f
Ki - mi - ga yo wa . Chi - yo - ni
May thy peace - ful reign last long! May it last for
Ya - chi - yo - ni Sa - za - ré - i - shi no, I - wa - o to
thou - sands of years, Un - til this ti - ny stone will grow in - to a
na - ri - té, Ko - ké no mu - su ma - dé.
mas - sive rock And the moss will cov - er it all deep and thick.

First performed on 3rd November, 1880, on the Emperor Meiji's birthday, and approved as National Anthem on 12th August, 1893.

JOHORE

Words written in 1914
in Malay by
Captain Haji Mohamed Said BIN H. SULIEMAN S.M.J.
in English by
H. A. COURTNEY

Music composed in 1879 by
M. GALISTAN,
Bandmaster of the
Johore Military Forces

mf
Al - lah pe - li - ha - ra - kan Sul - tan 'Nug -
God pre - serve the Sul - tan,
mf
rah - kan di - a se - ga - la ke - hor - ma - tan se -
Grant that ho - nour, health and hap - pi - ness may be
hat dan ri - a ke - kal dan ma' - mor. Lu - a - s
with him e - ver - more!

The music received the Assent of His Highness Sir Abu Bakar, Maharajah of Johore (afterwards Sultan of Johore) in 1879.
The words received the Assent of His Highness Sir Ibrahim, Sultan of Johore, in 1915.

kan kua - sa me - na - ung kan ka - mi Ra' -
Long may his hand pro - tect our land And
yat di - pim - pi - ni ber - za man la - gi De - ngan
lead his peo - ple on through years to be In
cresc.
mer - de - ka ber - sa - tu ha - ti Al - lah ber - ka - ti Jo - hor Al - lah
free - dom and in u - ni - ty. God bless Jo - hore!
cresc.
f
rit.
se - la - mat kan Sul - tan.
God save the Sul - tan!
rit.

JORDAN

Words by
Professor 'ABDULMUN 'IM AR-RIFAA'I

Music by
Professor ABDULKADIR AT-TANNIR

Largo ma non troppo
'A - sha al Ma - leek Sa - mi - yan ma - qa - mu - hu

Kha - fi - qa - tin_ fil ma - 'a - li_ a - 'lam - u - hu.

Free Translation

Long live the King
Long live the King
His position is sublime
His banners waving in glory supreme.

Adopted as National Anthem when Emir Abdullah became King, 25 May, 1946.

KEDAH

Maestoso
mf
Al - lah se - la - mat Sul - tan mah - ko - o -
mf
ta Ber - pan - ja-ngan u - sia di - a - tas takh -
mp
ta, Me - meli - ha - ra u - ga - ma na - bi ki - i -
mp

f
ta Ne - ge - ri Ke-dah se - ra - ta ra - ta.
f

Free Translation

God save our reigning Sultan,
Long live his reign,
To uphold the religion of our prophet,
Throughout the State of Kedah.

KELANTAN

Words by
TENGKU MAHMOOD MAHYIDEEN

Music by
INCHE MAHMOOD BIN HAMZAH

seh dan ta' - at di - sem - bah - kan sa - pe - noh. Ke - ri - a -
ngan pa - tek — u-chap - kan Se - ga - la ke - be - sa - ran Al - lah chu-chor
kan dar - jah ke - mu - lia - an Al - lah tam - bah - kan.
rit.
rit.

Free Translation

Long live our Sultan,
Sultan of Kelantan is our Royal King,
God bestow peace and prosperity upon him,
Forever he reigns over us,
Love and loyalty we fully pledged,
We pray for His happiness,
May the grace of God bestow honour and dignity upon him,
Forever by God's grace.

KENYA

Traditional Kenya melody

The first line of each verse, * to *, may be sung by a soloist in the African traditional style.

Firmly
1. *Ee Mu - ngu ngu - vu ye - tu* I - -le - te ba - ra - ka kwe - tu
2. A - m - ke - ni ndu - gu ze - tu Tu - -fa - nye so - te bi - dii
3. Na - tu - je - nge ta - i - fa le - tu Ee ndi - o wa - ji - bu we - tu
1. O God of all cre - a - tion Bless this our land and na - tion.
con Ped.
Ha - ki i - we nga - o na mli - nzi Na - tu -
Na - si tu - ji - to - e kwa ngu - vu Nch - i
Ken - ya i - sta - hil - i he - shi - ma Tu - u -
Just - ice be our shield and de - fend - er, May we

The Kenya National Anthem is based on a traditional Kenya Folk Song which was adapted and harmonized by a National Commission of Musicians who also wrote the words. This honorary Commission comprised Graham Hyslop, M.A., Dip. Mus.; George W. Senoga-Zake, L.R.S.M.; Peter Kibukosya; Thomas Kalume; and Washington Omondi.

-ka - e na u - du - gu A - ma - ni na u - hu - ru
ye - tu ya Ken - ya tu - na - yo - i - pe - nda
-nga - ne mi - ko - no pa - mo - ja ka - zi - ni
dwell in un - i - ty, Peace and lib - er - ty
1&2
3
Ra - ha tu - pa - te na u - sta - wi. 2. A - m-
Tu - we ta - ya - ri ku - i - li - nda. 3. Na-tu-
Ki - la si - ku tu - we na - shu- -kra - ni.
Plen - ty be found with - in our bor - ders.
(crescendo last verse.)

2. Let one and all arise
With hearts both strong and true.
Service be our earnest endeavour,
And our Homeland of Kenya,
Heritage of splendour,
Firm may we stand to defend.

3. Let all with one accord
In common bond united,
Build this our nation together,
And the glory of Kenya,
The fruit of our labour
Fill every heart with thanksgiving.

KOREA (NORTH)

Democratic Republic of Korea

Words by
PAK SE YONG

Music by
KIM WON GYUN

Fairly slowly and solemnly
mf
1 A ch'im ŭn pin - na - ra, i kang-san ŭn -
gum e, cha - wŏn do ka - dŭk han sam - ch'ŏl - li, a - rŭm-da - un
nae cho-guk, pan - man-nyŏn ora-en ryŏk-sa e ch'al - lan han mun-hwa ro
f
cha - ra - nan sŭl - gi - roun in - min ŭi i yŏng-gwang: Mom_
mp

Adopted in 1947 but no further information available.

gwa mam ta_ pa-ch'yŏ, i, cho-sŏn kir - i___ pat - tŭ - se. Ch'al- se.
1
2

2. Paektusan kisang ŭl ta anko.
kŭllo ŭi chŏngsin ŭn kittŭrŏ.
chilli ro mungch'yŏ jin ŏksen ttŭt
on segye apsŏ nagari.
Sonnŭn him nodo do naemirŏ,
inmin ŭi ttŭs ŭro sŏn nara.
Han ŏpsi pugang hanŭn
i chosŏn kiri pinnaese.

English Translation

1. Let morning shine on the silver and gold of this land,
three thousand leagues packed with natural wealth.
my beautiful fatherland,
the glory of a wise people
brought up in a culture brilliant
with a history five millenia long.
Let us devote our bodies and minds
to supporting this Korea for ever.

2. The firm will, bonded with truth,
nest for the spirit of labour,
embracing the atmosphere of Mount Paektu,
will go forth to all the world.
The country established by the will of the people,
breasting the raging waves with soaring strength.
Let us glorify for ever this Korea
limitlessly rich and strong.

English versification by
WHAMI KOH and
T. M. CARTLEDGE

KOREA (SOUTH)
Republic of Korea

Music by
EAKTAI AHN
(1906-1965)

Andante maestoso

ff

f

1. *Tong - hai Mool - kwa Paik - tu - san - i Ma - ru - go Tal - to -*
2. *Nam - san U - ye Chu - so - na - mu Chul - kap - eul Tur - ul -*
1. Tong - Hai Sea and Pak - doo Moun - tain, So long as they en -
2. E - ter - nal - ly Naam - saan's pine - trees Stand like an ar - mour

f

f

- rok Ha - na - nim - i Po - ho - ha - sa
- tut Pa - ram - i - sul Pul - byun - ha - mum
- dure, May God bless Ko - re - a our land For
sure, Through what - ev - er tem - pest or dan - ger,

f

Talt - to - rok
Tur - ul - tut
en - dure,
like ar - mour,

f

This song, of unknown authorship, was set originally to a different tune and sung in Korea for many years. When the Government of the Republic of Korea was established on 15th August, 1948, these verses, with the music by Eaktai Ahn, were officially adopted as the National Anthem.

CHORUS
U - ri na - ra Man - sei.
U - ri ki - sang Il - sae.
end - less a - ges to come!
As our sym - bol of strength.
Man - sei.
Il - sae.
end - less a - ges!
as our sym - bol.
Moo - gung - wha
North to South be -
Sam - chul - ri Hwa - ryu Kang - san,
- decked with flow - ers, Land of beau - ty rare,
Hwa - ryu Kang - san, Hwa - ryu - han.
land of beau - ty, land of beau - ty.
Tae - han Sa - ram Tae - han eu - ro Ki - ri Po - chun - ha - sae.
May God keep our coun - try u - nit - ed And pre - serve our land.

KUWAIT

No words

Music by
MOHAMMED YOUSUF OUWDIS

This is played on ceremonial occasions. It was adopted as the National Anthem in 1951.

LAOS

Words by
MAHA PHOUMI
English versification by
T. M. CARTLEDGE

Music by
S. E. THONGDY

f
Xad - lao tang - tè - deum - ma khung - xu - lu -
Once our La - o - tian race in A - sia
- xa you - ney - a - xy Xao - lao pouk - phan - mey -
high - ly hon - oured stood, And at that time the
p
- try houam - sa - ma - khy hak - ho - hom - kan. Hak -
folk of La - os were u - ni - ted in love. To -
mf
f

The music is reproduced by permission of Institut fur Auslands-beziehungen, Stuttgart, from *Die National-Hymnen Der Erde*.
Adopted as National Anthem, 1947. Written and first used 1941.

-xad hak-pa-thet-hao hak-tiao pok-két-ké-
-day they love their race and ral-ly round their
-sa. Hom-hak houam sat-sa-na tè-bou-hal-
chiefs, They guard the land and the re-li-gion
cresc.
f
ff
-ma hak-sa-din-dèn. Bo-hey xad-dey-ma-
of their an-ces-tors. They will re-sist each
cresc.
f
ff
p
-louan ra-vi-lop-kouan nhad-nheng-xing-ao: Phey-khun-
foe who may op-press them or in-vade And_
p

-khao ma - lou - voun - vay sou - choon - toua -
such in - vad - ers will be met with
mf
f
-tay tane - thane - sad - trou. Xouy-xeud - xou leuad-neua - xeua -
bat - tle un - to death. They'll re - store the fame of
mf
f
-phao fun - fou - kou - ao ban - hao - thouk - kan.
La - os and through ills u - nit - ed stand.

French Words

Notre race Lao a jadis connu en Asie une grande renommée.
Alors les Lao étaient unis et s'aimaient.
Aujourd'hui encore ils savent aimer leur race et leur pays et se groupent autour de leurs chefs.
Ils ont conservé la religion de leurs pères et ils savent garder le sol des aïeux.
Ils ne permettront pas que quelque nation vienne les troubler ou s'emparer de leur terre.
Quiconque voudrait envahir leur pays les trouverait résolus à combattre jusqu'à la mort.
Tous ensemble ils sauront restaurer l'antiquè gloire du sang lao et s'entr'aider aux jours d'épreuves.

LATVIA

Translated by
Dr. GEORGE A. SIMONS

Words and Music by
KARLIS BAUMANIS
(1834-1904)

f Maestoso
Dievs, svē - ti Lat - vi - ju, mūs' dār - go
Bless Lat - vi - a, O God, Our ver - dant
f

tē - vi - ju, svē - ti jel Lat - vi - ju, ak
na - tive sod. Where Bal - tic he - roes trod,

1
2
mf
svē - ti jel to! to! Kur lat - vju
Keep her from harm! harm! Our love - ly
mf

Originally written as an entry for a singing festival in 1873, it very soon became the National Anthem
Since 1940 the National Anthem of the U.S.S.R. has been sung inside Latvia.

cresc.
mei - tas zied, kur lat - vju dē - li dzied,
daugh - ters near, Our sing - ing sons ap - pear,
cresc.
f
laid mums tur lai - mē diet, mūs
May For - tune smil - ing here
f
1
2
Lat - vi - jā.
Grace Lat - vi - a.
Lat - vi - jā.
Grace Lat - vi - a!

LEBANON

Words by
RACHID NAKHLÉ (d. 1939)

Music by
WADIA SABRA
(1876-1952)

Martial
f

sf
sf
3

f
1. Koul-lou-na lil-oua-tann Lil-'ou-la lil 'a
2. Chay-khou-na oual-fa-ta in-da-saôu-til oua
3. Bah-rou-hou bar-rou-hou Dour-ra-touch-char

Adopted officially by
Presidential decree on 12th Jul, 1927

lam, Mil - ou 'ay niz - za - man Say - fou - na oual ka -
tann Ous - dou ghâ bin ma - ta Sa - oua - rat nal - fi -
kain Ril - dou - hou bir - rou - hou Ma - li - oul kout -
3

p
- lam, Sah - lou - na oual - ja - bal man - bi
- tann Char - kou - na kal - bou - hou a - ba
- baïn is - mou - hou 'iz - zou - hou moun zou
3
p

tonn lir - ri - jâl, Kaou - lou - na oual 'a - mal Fi - sa
dann loub - nane Sa - na - hou rab bou - hou Li - ma -
kâ - nal jou - doude Maj - dou - hu ar - zou - hou Ram - zou -

Free Translation

1. All of us! For our Country, for our Flag and Glory!
Our valour and our writings are the envy of the ages.
Our mountains and our valleys, they bring forth stalwart men.
And to Perfection all our efforts we devote.
All of us! For our Country, for our Flag and Glory!

2. Our Elders and our children, they await our Country's call:
And on the Day of Crisis they are as Lions of the Jungle.
The heart of our East is ever Lebanon:
May God preserve her until end of time.
All of us! For our Country, for our Flag and Glory!

3. The Gems of the East are her land and sea.
Throughout the world her good deeds flow from pole to pole.
And her name is her glory since time began.
Immortality's Symbol- the Cedar- is her Pride
All of us! For our Country, for our Flag and Glory!

LESOTHO

Words by
FRANÇOIS COILLARD

Music by L. LAUR
(19th century)

mf
1. Le - so - tho fa - tŝe la bo - nta - t'a ro - na, Ha - r'a ma - fa - tŝe le le - tle ke lo - na.
f
Ke moo re hla - hi - leng, Ke moo re ho - li - leng, Re - a le ra - ta.
Ha - r'a ma - fa - tŝe le le - tle ke lo - na.
Ke moo re hla - hi - leng, Ke moo re ho - li - leng, Re - a le ra - ta.

2. *Molimo ak'u boloke Lesotho,*
U felise lintoa le matŝoenyeho.
Oho fatŝe lena,
La bo-ntat'a rona,
Le be le khotso.

1. Lesotho, land of our Fathers,
You are the most beautiful country of all.
You give us birth,
In you we are reared
And you are dear to us.

2. Lord, we ask You to protect Lesotho.
Keep us free from conflict and tribulations.
Oh, land of mine,
Land of our Fathers,
May you have peace.

The Government adopted this as their National Anthem on 2nd May, 1967, using the first and last verses of the words written by a French missionary.

LIBERIA

Words by
DANIEL BASHER WARNER* (b. 1815)

Music by
OLMSTEAD LUCA

Moderato
f
1. All hail, Li-be-ria, hail! All hail, Li-be-ria, hail! This glo-rious land of li-ber-ty Shall long be ours Though new her name, Green be her fame, And
2. All hail, Li-be-ria, hail! All hail, Li-be-ria, hail! In u-nion strong suc-cess is sure— We can-not fail! With God a-bove Our rights to prove We
f
cresc.

*Third President of Liberia, 1864-1868

migh - ty be her pow'rs
will o'er all pre - vail!
And migh - ty be her pow'rs
We will o'er all pre - vail!
p
In
With
p

joy and glad - ness With our hearts u - ni - ted, We'll shout the
heart and hand Our coun-try's cause de-fend - ing We'll meet the
ff
free - dom Of a race be-night - ed,
foe With va-lour un-pre-tend - ing.
Long live Li - be - ria,
ff
hap - py land! A home of glo-rious li-ber-ty, By God's com -
- mand! A home of glo-rious li - ber-ty, By God's com - mand!

LIBYAN ARAB REPUBLIC

Words by
A. SHAMSEDDEIN *

Music by
M. CHAREIF

Libya became a republic in September 1969. *It has not been possible to obtain the words.

LIECHTENSTEIN

Words by
H. H. JAUCH (1850)

Composer unknown

Moderato
mf
1. O - ben am deut - schen Rhein leh - net sich Liech - ten-stein
2. Wo einst Sankt Lu - zi - en Frie - den nach Rä - ti - en
mf
an Al - pen - höh'n.
hin - ein ge - bracht,
f
Dies lie - be Hei - mat-land im deut - schen
dort an dem Gren - zen-stein und längs dem
f
Va - ter-land hat Got - tes__ wei - se Hand für uns er - seh'n.
jun - gen Rhein steht furcht-los__ Liech - ten-stein auf Deutschlands Wacht.
ff
ff

The tune is the same as that of the National Anthem of Great Britain.

3. *Lieblich zur Sommerzeit*
Auf hoher Alpenweid
Schwebt Himmelsruh,
Wo frei die Gemse springt,
Kühn sich der Adler schwingt,
Der Senn' das Ave singt
Der Heimat zu.

4. *Von grüngen Felsenhöhn*
Freundlich ist es zu sehn
Mit einem Blick,
Wie des Rheines Silberband
Säumet das schöne Land,
Ein kleines Vaterland
Voll stillen Glücks.

5. *Hoch lebe Liechtenstein,*
Blühend am deutschen Rhein,
Glücklich und treu.
Hoch leb der Fürst vom Land,
Hoch unser Vaterland,
Durch Bruderliebe Band
Vereint und frei.

Free Translation

1. High above the German Rhine
leans Liechtenstein
against Alpine slopes.
This beloved homeland
in the German fatherland
was chosen for us by
the Lord's wisdom.

2. Where once St. Lucius
brought peace to Rätien,
there on the boundary-stone
and along the young Rhine
stands dauntless Liechtenstein
on Germany's guard.

3. Lovely in summer-time
on high Alpine pastures
floats heavenly peace,
where the chamois freely jumps about,
the eagle sways boldy in the air,
the herdsman sings the 'Ave'
towards the homeland.

4. From high green rocks
it is a lovely sight to watch
how the silvery ribbon of the Rhine
edges the beautiful country,
a small fatherland,
full of quiet happiness.

5. Long live Liechtenstein,
blossoming on the German Rhine,
happy and faithful.
Long live the Duke of the Land,
Long live our fatherland,
united by brotherly bonds and free.

LITHUANIA

Words and Music by
VINCAS KUDIRKA (1858-1899)

Maestoso
f
1. Lie - tu-va, tė - vy-nė mū-sų tu did-vy-rių
2. Te - gul ta-vo vai-kai ei-na vien ta-kais do -
že - mė Iš pra-ei-ties ta-vo sū-nūs
ry - bės! Te - gul dir-ba ta-vo nau-dai
1
2
te sti-pry-bę se - mia! ir - žmo-nių gė - ry - bes!
pp cresc.
1. Te - gul sau-lė Lie - tu-vos tam - su-mus pra -
2. Te - gul mei-lė Lie - tu-vos de - ga mū - sų
pp cresc.

This became the National Anthem 1918 and first appeared in print in 1896
In Lithuania the National Anthem of the U.S.S.R. is now used.

3. *Tegul saulė Lietuvos*
Tamsumus prašalina,
Ir šviesa, ir tiesa
Mūs žingsnius telydi.

4. *Tegul meilė Lietuvos*
Dega mūsų širdyse,
Vardan tos Lietuvos
Vienybė težydi!

1. Lithuania, land of heroes,
Thou our Fatherland that art,
From the glorious deeds of ages
Shall Thy children take heart.

2. May Thy children ever follow
Their heroic fathers
In devotion to their country
And good will to others.

3. May the sun of our loved shore
Shine upon us evermore;
May the right and the truth
Keep our pathway lighted.

4. May the love of our dear land
Make us strong of heart and hand,
May our land ever stand
Peaceful and united.

LUXEMBOURG

Ons Hémécht

OUR MOTHERLAND

Words by
MICHAEL LENTZ
(1820-1893)
Translated by
NICHOLAS E. WEYDERT

Music by
J. A. ZINNEN
(1827-1898)
Arr. by MARTIN SHAW
(1875-1958)

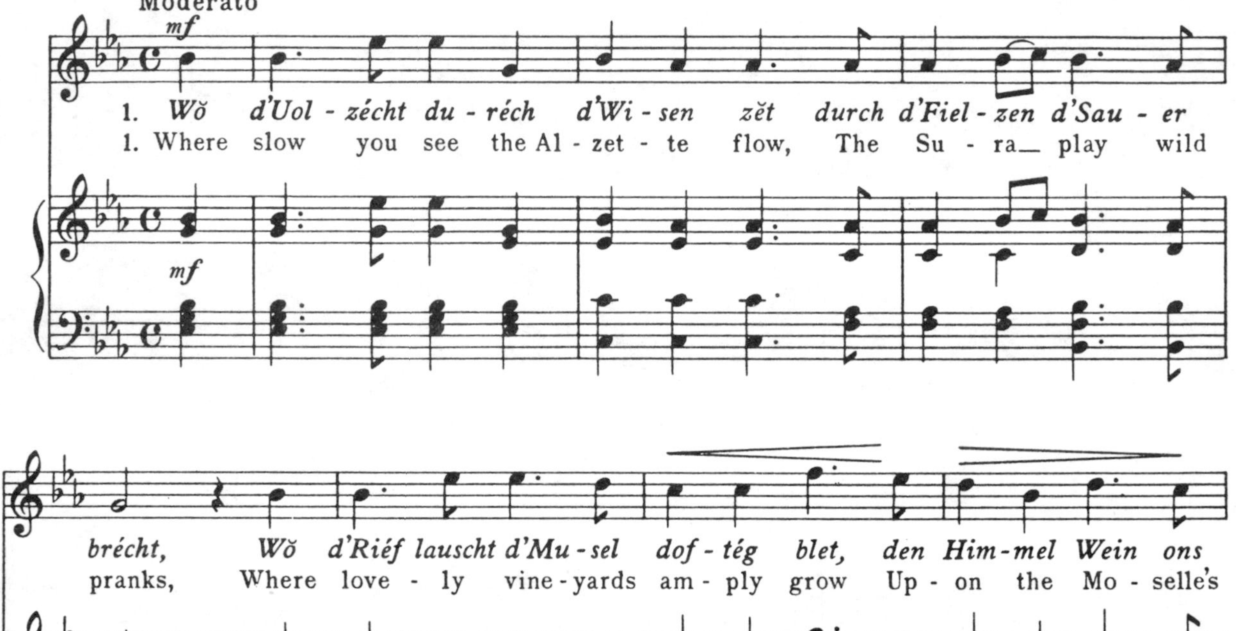
Moderato
mf
1. Wŏ d'Uol - zécht du - réch d'Wi - sen zĕt durch d'Fiel - zen d'Sau - er
1. Where slow you see the Al - zet - te flow, The Su - ra_ play wild
mf

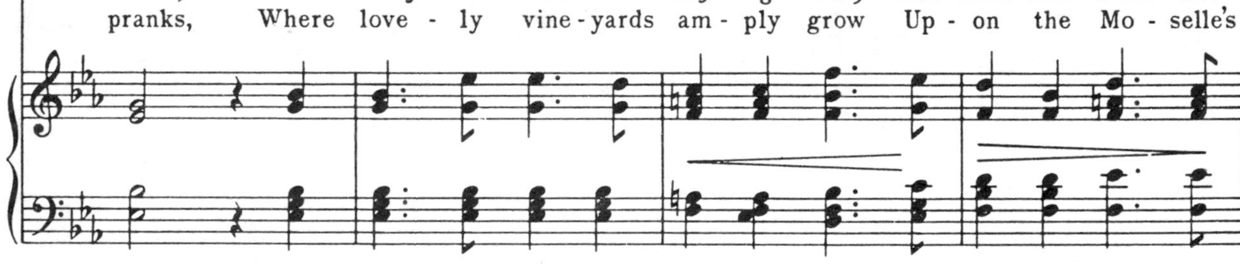
brécht, Wŏ d'Riéf lauscht d'Mu - sel dof - tég blet, den Him - mel Wein ons
pranks, Where love - ly vine - yards am - ply grow Up - on the Mo - selle's

p
mécht; Dât ass ons Land fir dât mer gĕf hei -
banks, There lies the land for which our thanks Are
p

First performed 5th June, 1864, this became the National Anthem in 1895 replacing *De Feierwon* (The Festal Train) by the same author (a well-known poet) and composer. *De Feierwon* was written in 1859 to celebrate the opening of the first international railway system connecting the Grand Duchy with the outside world. It is still a popular hymn in Luxembourg.

f
mf
-ni - den al - les w'on, onst Hé - méchts-land dât
owed to God a - bove, Our own, our— na - tive
f
mf
f
mir sŏ dĕf an on - sen Hier - zer dro'n. Onst
land which ranks Well fore - most in our love. Our
f
Hé - méchts-land dât mir sŏ dĕf an on - sen Hier - zer dro'n!
own, our na - tive land which ranks Well fore most in our love.

2. *O Du do uewen, dém seng Hand*
Durch d'Welt d'Natio'ne lêd,
Behitt Du d'Letzeburger Land
Vum friéme Joch a Lêd.
Du hues ons all als Kanner schon
De freie Gêscht jo gin;
LôB viru blénken d'Freihêtssonn,
De' mir 'so' lâng gesin.
LôB viru blénken d'Freihêtssonn,
De' mir 'so' lâng gesin.

2. Oh Father in Heaven Whose powerful hand
Makes states or lays them low,
Protect the Luxembourger land
From foreign yoke and woe.
God's golden liberty bestow
On us now as of yore.
Let Freedom's sun in glory glow
For now and evermore.

MALACCA

Arranged by
W. L. REED

Free Translation

Malacca, the State of Malacca,
The land of our birth,
We honour with our lives,
For progress and success,
The subjects are united
To pledge their loyalty,
Serving sincerely all the time.
Progress and success for Malacca.

MALAGASY REPUBLIC

O, Our Beloved Fatherland

Words by P. RAHAJASON

Music by
NORBERT RAHARISOA
Arr. by HENRY COLEMAN

This National Anthem was adopted on 21st October, 1958 by Madagascar.
The name of the country was changed to the Malagasy Republic on 26th June, 1960.

CHORUS
-hi - onao ry Za-na-ha - ry 'Ty No - si-ndrazanay i-
-ty Hi - a - da-na sy ho fi - na - ri-tra He
sa-mba-tra to-koa i - za - hay Ta hay.
f
f
1
2
p
p

1. O, our beloved fatherland,
   O, fair Madagascar,
   Our love will never decay
   But will last eternally.

2. O, our beloved fatherland,
   Let us be thy servant
   With body, heart and spirit
   In dear and worthy service.

3. O, our beloved fatherland,
   May God bless thee,
   That created all lands;
   In order He maintains thee.

CHORUS O, Lord Creator do Thou bless
This Island of our Fathers
That she may be happy and prosperous
For our own satisfaction.

MALAWI

O God bless Malawi

Words* and Music by
MICHAEL-FRED P. SAUKA
(b. 1934)

p
mf
1. O God bless our land of Ma - la - wi,
1. Mlu - ngu da - li - tsa - ni Ma - la - wi,
1. Chi - u - ta mtu - mbi - ke Ma - la - wi,
Keep it a land of peace.
Mum - su - nge m'mte - nde - re.
Mu - mu - pe mu - te - nde.
f
Put down each and every e - ne - my,
Go - nje - tsa - ni a - da - ni o - nse,
Mu - the - re - ske ba - rwa - ni wo - se,
ff
Hung - er, dis - ease, en - vy.
Nja - la, nthe - nda, nsa - nje.
Nja - ra, nthe - nda, sa - nje.

*The official text is given in English, Chinyanja and Chitumbuka.

This National Anthem was selected as a result of a competition held at the Malawi Headquarters in Zomba in February 1964. It was first played publicly on Independence Day, 6 July 1964.

mf
Join to - ge - ther all our hearts as one,
Lu - nzi - tsa - ni mi - ti - ma ya - thu,
Gu - ma - nya - ni mi - ti - ma yi - thu,
mf
f
That we be free from fear. Bless our lead - er,
Ku - ti ti - sa - o - pe. Mda - li - tse Mtso -
Nkhu - mbi ti - ba - vye - so. Mtu - mbi - ke Mlo -
f
f
p
mf rit.
pp
each and ev - ery one, And Mo - ther Ma - la - wi.
- go le - ri na - fe, Ndi Ma - i Ma - la - wi.
- ngo - zgi na - to - se, Na ma - ma Ma - la - wi.
p
mf rit.
pp

ENGLISH

2. Our own Malawi, this land so fair,
Fertile and brave and free.
With its lakes, refreshing mountain air,
How greatly blest are we.
Hills and valleys, soil so rich and rare,
Give us a bounty free.
Wood and forest, plains so broad and fair,
All beauteous Malawi.

3. Freedom ever, let us all unite,
To build up Malawi.
With our love, our zeal and loyalty,
Bringing our best to her.
In time of war, or in time of peace,
One purpose and one goal.
Men and women serving selflessly,
In building Malawi.

CHINYANJA

2. *Malawi ndziko lokongola,*
La chonde ndi ufulu,
Nyanja ndi mphepo ya m'mapiri,
Ndithudi tadala.
Zigwa, mapiri, nthaka, dzinthu,
N'mphatso zaulere.
Nkhalango, madambo abwino.
Ngwokoma Malawi.

3. *O! Ufulu tigwirizane,*
Kukweza Malawi.
Ndi chikondi, khama, kumvera,
Timutumikire.
Pa nkhondo nkana pa mtendere,
Cholinga n'chimodzi.
Mai, bambo, tidzipereke,
Pokweza Malawi.

CHITUMBUKA

2. *Malawi charo chakutowa,*
Nyata na wanangwa,
Nyanja, mphepo za mumapiri.
Ta ba mwabi ndise,
M'madambo nthaka ya vundira,
Vyatipa wanangwa.
Nguyi na madambo ghaweme,
Kutowa Malawi.

3. *Wanangwa muyaya pamoza,*
Tizenge Malawi.
Kutemwa na mwamphu na nchindi
Timutebetere.
Mnyengo ya nkhondo nesi mtende,
Chikhomo chimoza.
Mama, dada, mwe tijipate,
Mkukuzga Malawi.

MALAYSIA

NEGARA KU

MY COUNTRY

Words compiled by
a special Committee

Melody derived from
old Malay folk tune

Maestoso
mf
Ne - ga - ra ku Ta - nah tum-pah - nya
mf

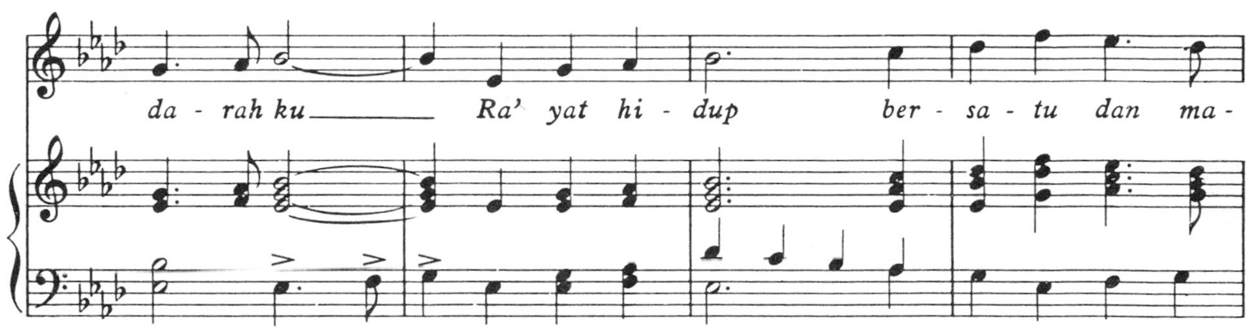
da - rah ku Ra' yat hi - dup ber - sa - tu dan ma -

A
f
- ju Rah-mat bah - gia tu - han kur-ni - a
f

For short version cut from A to B

Adopted as National Anthem when Malaya achieved Independence on 31st August, 1957. It was previously known in Malaya and Indonesia as a popular song called Terang Bulan (Moonlight): but this popular version of the tune is now banned. When Malaysia was founded in 1963 this was retained as the National Anthem.

kan
Ra - ja ki - ta se - la - mat ber - takh -
B
ff
ta
Rah-mat bah - gia tu - han kur-ni - a kan
ff
molto rall.
Ra - ja ki - ta se - la - mat ber - takh - ta.
molto rall.

Free Translation

My Country,
The land of my birth.
May her people live in unity and prosperity,
May God grant His blessings upon her,
Peacefully may our Ruler reign.
May God grant His blessings upon her,
Peacefully may our Ruler reign.

MALDIVES REPUBLIC

Words by
MOHAMED JAMEEL DIDI

Music by
W. A. AMERADEVA
Arr. by T. M. CARTLEDGE

This was adopted on 13 March, 1972, replacing the former national anthem.

Transliteration

Gavmii mi ekuverikan matii tibegen kuriime salaam,
Gavmii bahun gina heyo du'aa kuramun kuriime salaam.
Gavmii nishaanang hurmataa eku boo lambai tibegen
Audaanakan libigen e vaa dida-ak kuriime salaam.
Nasraa nasiibaa kaamyaabu-ge ramzakang himenee
Fessaa rataai hudaa ekii fenumun kuriime salaam.
Fakhraa sharaf gavmang e hoodai devvi batalunna'
Zikraage mativeri ŧentakun adugai kuriime salaam.
Divehiinge ummay kuri arai silmaa salaamatugai
Divehiinge nan moŧu vun adai tibegen kuriime salaam.
Minivankamaa madaniyyataa libigen mi 'aalamugai
Dinigen hitaama tibun edigen kuriime salaam.
Diinaai takhtang heyo hitun hurmay adaa kuramun
Siidaa vafaaterikan matii tibegen kuriime salaam.
Davlatuge aburaa 'izzataa mativeri vegen abada'
Audaana vun edi heyo du'aa kuramun kuriime salaam.

English Translation

We salute you in this national unity.
We salute you, with many good wishes in the national tongue,
Bowing the head in respect to the national symbol.
We salute the flag that has such might;
It falls into the sphere of victory, fortune and success
With its green and red and white together, and therefore we salute it.
To those heroes who sought out honour and pride for the nation
We give salute to-day in auspicious verses of remembrance.
May the nation of the Maldivian Islanders advance under guard and protection
And the name of the Maldivian Islanders become great. Thus we pledge as we salute.
We wish for their freedom and progress in this world
And for their freedom from sorrows, and thus we salute.
With full respect and heartfelt blessing towards religion and throne
We salute you in uprightness and truth.
May the State ever have auspicious honour and respect.
With good wishes for your continuing might, we salute you.

MALI

Music by
BANZOUMANA SISSOKO
Arr. by HENRY COLEMAN

This National Anthem was adopted by the National Assembly of Mali on 9th August 1962

- parts Nous som - mes ré - so - lus de mou - rir.
Chorus
Pour l'A - frique et pour toi MA - LI
- LI au - jour - d'hui O MA - LI de de - main Les champs fleu -
rall. 2nd time
No - tre dra - peau se - ra li - ber - té.
- ris - sent d'es - pé - ran - ce, Les coeurs vi - brent de con -
rall. 2nd time
1
Pour l'A - frique et pour toi MA - LI

2
No - tre com - bat se - ra u - ni - té. O MA- fian - ce.

2. *Debout, villes et campagnes,*
Debout, femmes, jeunes et vieux
Pour la Patrie en marche
Vers l'avenir radieux
Pour notre dignité.
Renforçons bien nos rangs,
Pour le salut public
Forgeons le bien commun
Ensemble, au coude à coude
Faisons le chantier du bonheur.

3. *La voie est dure, très dure*
Qui mène au bonheur commun.
Courage et dévouement, } (bis.)
Vigilance à tout moment,
Vérité des temps anciens,
Vérité de tous les jours,
Le bonheur par le labeur
Fera le MALI de demain.

4. *L'Afrique se lève enfin*
Saluons ce jour nouveau.
Saluons la liberté,
Marchons vers l'unité.
Dignité retrouvée
Soutient notre combat.
Fidèles à notre serment
De faire l'Afrique unie
Ensemble, debout mes frères
Tous au rendez-vous de l'honneur.

English Translation by
T.M. CARTLEDGE

1. At your call, MALI,
So that you may prosper,
Faithful to your destiny,
We shall all be united,
One people, one goal, one faith
For a united Africa.
If the enemy should show himself
Within or without,
On the ramparts
We are ready to stand and die.

Chorus For Africa and for you, MALI,
Our banner shall be liberty.
For Africa and for you, MALI,
Our fight shall be for unity.
Oh, MALI of today,
Oh, MALI of tomorrow,
The fields are flowering with hope
And hearts are thrilling with confidence.

2. Stand up, towns and countryside,
Stand up, women, stand up young and old,
For the Fatherland on the road
Towards a radiant future.
For the sake of our dignity
Let us strengthen our ranks;
For the public well-being
Let us forge the common good.
Together, shoulder to shoulder,
Let us work for happiness.

3. The road is hard, very hard,
That leads to common happiness.
Courage and devotion,
Constant vigilance,
Courage and devotion,
Constant vigilance,
Truth from olden times,
The truths of every day,
Happiness through effort
Will build the MALI of tomorrow.

4. Africa is at last arising,
Let us greet this new day.
Let us greet freedom,
Let us march towards unity.
Refound dignity
Supports our struggle.
Faithful to our oath
To make a united Africa,
Together, arise, my brothers,
All to the place where honour calls.

MALTA

Innu Malti

HYMN OF MALTA

Words by
DUN KARM PSAILA (1871-1961)
Translated by
MAY BUTCHER

Music by
ROBERT SAMMUT
(1870 -1934)

Dun Karm Psaila, Malta's greatest poet, was asked to write these words for a school hymn to Sammut's music. He conceived the idea of writing a hymn to Malta in the form of a prayer; he wanted to unite all parties with the strong ties of religion and love of country.
It was first performed on 3rd February, 1923, and later declared to be the official anthem (on 7th April, 1941).

land so dear whose name we bear!
-lej, Kif dej - jem Int ha - rist:
mer - cy, strength in man in - crease!
-na lis - sid, sah - ha 'l - had - di - em.
f
Keep her in mind whom Thou hast made so fair!
Fta - kar li lil - ha bil - oh - la dawl lib - bist!
Con - firm us all in u - ni - ty and peace!
Sed - daq il - ghaq - da fil - Mal - tin u s - sliem!
f

MAURITANIA

No words

Based on traditional music, this was adopted as the National Anthem in 1960, the year of Independence.

secco
1. For continuation
2. Fine
f poco pesante
sempre f
simile

come sopra
Ped. Ped.
simile
eome sopra
Ped. Ped. Ped. Ped.
simile
D. 𝄋 al Fine

MAURITIUS

Motherland

Words by
JEAN GEORGES PROSPER

Music by
PHILIPPE GENTIL

This National Anthem, which was selected by means of a competition, came into use when Mauritius attained Independence on 12 March 1968.

It is played after the National Anthem for Great Britain when Her Majesty the Queen or her special representative (not including the Governor-General) is present, or when musical honours accompany the Royal Toast at a State Dinner.

ff
one peo-ple, As one na-tion, For peace, jus-tice and li-ber-
ff
ty. Be-lov-ed coun-try, may
mf
mf
cresc. e poco a poco rall.
God bless thee For e-ver and e-ver.
ff
cresc. e poco a poco rall.
ff

MEXICO

Words by
FRANCISCO GONZÁLEZ BOCANEGRA
(1824-1861)
Translated by
Miss B. ROMERO
Versified by
J.E. HALES

Music by
JAIME NUNÓ
(1824-1908)

Marziale
ff CHORUS

pp

1. *Me - xi - ca - nos al gri - to_ de gue - - rra El a -*
1. Mex - i - cans, when the trum - pet_ is call - - ing, Grasp your

ff *pp*

- ce - ro ap - res - tad y el bri - dón.......... Y re -
sword and your har - ness as - sem - ble. Let the

- tiem - ble en sus cen - tros la tie - rra, Al so -
guns with their thun - der ap - pal - ling Make the

Poem first performed 16th September, 1854, at the National Theatre in Mexico, to a different setting. Later the poem, set to Nunó's music, was selected through a government competition.

-no - ro ru-gir del ca - ñón, Y re-
Earth's deep foun-da - tions to trem - ble. Let the
-tiem - ble en sus cen - tros la tie - - - rra al so-
guns with their thun - der ap - pal - - - ling Make the
Fine
-no - ro ru-gir del ca - ñón.
Earth's deep foun-da - tions to trem - ble.
ff
Fine

VERSE
Ci-ña ¡Oh pa - tria! tus sie - nes de o - li - - - va De la
May the an - gel di - vine, O dear Home - - - land, Crown thy
paz el ar - cán - gel di - vi - - no Que en el
brow with the o - live branch of peace; For thy
cie - lo tu e - ter - no des - ti - no Por el
des - ti - ny, traced by God's own hand In the
de - - do de Dios se es - cri - bió Mas si o -
hea - - vens, shall e - ver in - crease. But should

-sa - re un ex-tra - ño e - ne - mi - go Pro - fa-
e - ver the proud foe as - sail thee, And with
-nar con su plan - ta tu sue - - - lo Pien - sa ¡Oh
in - so - lent foot pro - fane thy ground, Know, dear
pa - tria que - ri - da! que el cie - - - - lo Un sol-
Coun - try, thy sons shall not fail thee, Ev - 'ry
-da - do en ca - da hi - jo te dió Un sol -
one thy sol - dier shall be found, Thy sol - dier

D.C.
-da-do en ca-da hi-jo te diō.
ev-'ry one shall be found.
ff
D.C.

2. *¡Patria! ¡Patria! Tus hijos te juran*
Exhalar en tus aras su aliento,
Si el clarín, con su bélico acento,
Los convoca a lidiar con valor.
¡Para ti las guirnaldas de oliva!
¡Un recuerdo para ellos de gloria!
¡Un laurel para ti de victoria!
¡Un sepulcro para ellos de honor!

CORO: Mexicanos, etc.

2. Blessed Homeland, thy children have vowed them
If the bugle to battle should call,
They will fight with the last breath allowed them
Till on thy loved altars they fall.
Let the garland of olive thine be;
Unto them be deathless fame;
Let the laurel of victory be assigned thee,
Enough for them the tomb's honoured name.

CHORUS: Mexicans, etc.

MONACO

Words by
THÉOPHILE BELLANDO DE CASTRO (1820-1903)

Music by
ALBRECHT (1817-1895)
Arr. by HENRY COLEMAN

Performed for the first time in 1867 as a National Anthem. The music is based on a folk song used to Bellando's words as a marching song by the Guarde Nationale, in which Bellando served as a captain.

2. *Fiers Compagnons de la Garde Civique,*
Respectons tous la voix du Commandant.
Suivons toujours notre bannière antique.
Le tambour bat, marchons tous en Avant. (bis)

3. *Oui, Monaco connut toujours des braves.*
Nous sommes tous leurs dignes descendants.
En aucun temps nous ne fûmes esclaves,
Et loin de nous, régnèrent les tyrans. (bis)

4. *Que le nom d'un Prince plein de clémence*
Soit repété par mille et mille chants.
Nous mourons tous pour sa propre défense,
Mais après nous, combattrons nos enfants. (bis)

1. Principality of Monaco, my country,
Oh! how God is lavish with you.
An ever-clear sky, ever-blossoming shores,
Your Sovereign is better liked than a King. (repeat)

2. Proud Fellows of the Civic Guard,
Let us all listen to the Commander's voice.
Let us always follow our ancient flag.
Drums are beating, let us all march forward. (repeat)

3. Yes, Monaco always had brave men.
We all are their worthy descendants.
We never were slaves,
And far from us ruled the tyrants. (repeat)

4. Let the name of a Prince full of clemency
Be repeated in thousands and thousands of songs.
We shall all die in his defence,
But after us, our children will fight. (repeat)

MONGOLIA

No words

It has not been possible to obtain any information about the history of this National Anthem.

MOROCCO

Hymne Cherifien

No words

This version conforms to the orchestration approved by Si Mohammed Ben Youssef, Sultan of Morocco.
Arranged by LÉO MORGAN

p
ff
p
pp
RYTHME
Tebel
G. Caisse
id.
id.

MOZAMBIQUE PEOPLE'S REPUBLIC

Arranged by
W. L. REED

Martial (♩=120)
f
mf
1. Vi - va, vi - va a FRE - LI - MO, Gui -
a do Po - vo Mo - çam - bi - ca - no!
Po - vo he - ró - i - co qu'ar - ma em
mf

pun - ho O co - lo - nia - lis - mo der - ru - bou.
To - do o Po - vo u -
ni - do Des - de o Ro - vu - ma a - té - o Ma - pu - to,
Lu - ta contr - a im - pe - ria - lis - mo Con - ti - nua e sem - pre ven - ce -
ra.
CHORUS
Vi va Mo - çam - bi - que!

ff > f
Vi - va a Ban-dei - ra, sim - bo - lo Na - cio-nal! Vi - va Mo - çam-
ff > f
(rall. 2nd time)
1
2
bi - que! Que por ti o Po - vo lu - ta - rá. rá.
(rall. 2nd time)

Verse 2 Unido ao mundo inteiro,
Lutando contra a burguesia,
Nossa Pátria será túmulo
Do capitalismo e exploraçao.
O Povo Moçambicano
D'operários e de camponeses,
Engajado no trabalho
A riqueza sempre brotará.

English Translation

Verse 1 Viva viva FRELIMO
Guide of the Mozambican people,
Heroic people who, gun in hand,
toppled colonialism.
All the People united
From the Rovuma to the Maputo,
Struggle against imperialism
And continue, and shall win.

Verse 2 United with the whole world,
Struggling against the bourgeoisie,
Our country will be the tomb
Of capitalism and exploitation.
The Mozambican People,
Workers and peasants,
Engaged in work
Shall always produce wealth.

Chorus Viva Mozambique,
Viva our flag, symbol of the Nation,
Viva Mozambique
For thee your People will fight.

NAURU

Music by
L. H. HICKS (b.1912)

Nauru obtained independence on 31 January 1968. The music was composed by Squadron Leader L.H. Hicks of the Royal Australian Airforce shortly before then. There are no official words as yet.

NEGRI SEMBILAN

Alla marcia
mf
Ber - kat - lah yang di - per - tu - an be - sar di - ne - ge - ri Sem -
mf
bi - lan. Kur - niai se - hat dan ma'a - mor,
Ka - sehi ra'a - yat lan - jutkan u - mor.
A - kan ber - kat - ı sa -

k'lian yang se - ti - a Mu - soh - nya
ha - bis, bi - na - sa, Be - r - kat - lah yang di - per - tuan be -
marcato
sar di - ne - ge - ri Sem - bi - lan.
marcato

Free Translation

Bless the great among the equal,
In Negri Sembilan.
Grant him health and prosperity,
Long life and the love of his subjects.
Bless those who are loyal.
His enemies shall be destroyed.
Bless the great among the equal in Negri Sembilan.

NEPAL

NATIONAL ANTHEM FOR
H.M. THE MAHARAJA DHIRAJA

Andante
f
Shri mân gum - bhi - ra ne - pâ - li pra-chan-da pra-tâ -
f
- pi bhu - pa-ti Shri pânch sar - kâr ma - hâ - râ -
ff
- jâ - dhi-râ - ja ko sa- dâ ra - hos un - na-ti Ra -
ff

-khun chi râ - yu ee - sha - le pra - jâ phai -
- li - yos pu-kâ - raun ja - ya pre - ma - le Hâ -
rall.
3
-mi ne - pâ - li bhâ - ee sâ - râ - le.
rall.
3

Free Translation

May glory crown you, courageous Sovereign, you,
the gallant Nepalese,
Shri Pansh Maharajadhiraja, our glorious ruler.
May he live for many years to come and may the
number of his subjects increase.
Let every Nepalese sing this with joy.

NETHERLANDS

Wilhelmus van Nassouwe

Words by
PHILIP MARNIX van St. ALDEGONDE
(1540-1598)
(Official Netherlands Government translation)

Composer unknown

Allegro risoluto
1. Wil - hel - mus van Nas - sou - we Ben ick van
1. Wil - liam of Nas - sau, sci - on of Dutch and

Duit - schen bloet; Den Va - der - lant ghe -
an - cient line, I de - di - cate un -

- trou - we Blijf ick tot in den doet. Een
- dy - ing faith to this land of mine. A

Composer unknown: melody known from before 1572.
Song appeared in Valerius' "Gedenck-Clanck", 1626.
It has 15 verses in all.

prin - ce van O - ran - jen Ben ick
Prince am I, un - daunt - ed, of
vrij on - ver - veert; Den Co - ninck
O - range e'er free, To the King of
van His - pan - jen Heb ick al - tijd ghe - eert.
Spain I've gran - ted a life's loy - al - ty.

2. *Mijn schilt en de betrouwen*
Sijt ghij, O Godt mijn Heer,
Op u soo wil ick bouwen
Verlaet mij nimmermeer!
Dat ick doch vroom mach blijven
U dienaer t'aller stondt,
Die Tyranny verdrijven,
Die mij mijn hert doorwondt.

2. My shield and my protection
Art Thou my Lord and God.
On Thee I build mine action,
Be evermore my rod.
That I be Thine eternal
And serve Thee fair and true
To chase tyrants infernal
Who my heart undo.

NETHERLANDS ANTILLES

Melody by
J. B. A. PALM (1885-1963)
Harmonised by
F. H. van AANHOLT

No words

Moderato

f

There are at present no words to this National Anthem. The composer is the conductor of the Police Force Band, and this Band played it for the first time as a National Anthem on the second lustrum of the celebration of the Charter on 15 December 1964. It had been used in the past for some considerable time as the anthem of the island territory of Bonaire.

The Netherlands National Anthem, which is used with it, is usually played at the beginning of ceremonies and the Netherlands Antilles Anthem at the end.

NEWFOUNDLAND

Words by
CHARLES CAVENDISH BOYLE
(1849-1916)

Music by
C. HUBERT H. PARRY
(1848-1918)
Arr. by HENRY COLEMAN

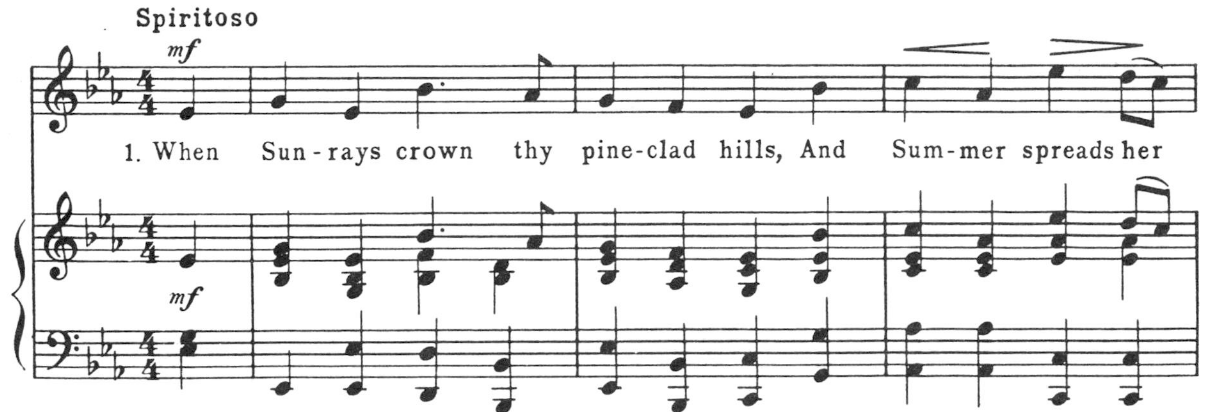
Spiritoso
mf
1. When Sun-rays crown thy pine-clad hills, And Sum-mer spreads her
mf

cresc.
hand, When sil - vern voi - ces tune thy rills We
cresc.

allargando
a tempo
f
love thee smil - ing land, We love thee, we
allargando
f
a tempo

Sir Charles Cavendish Boyle wrote the words when he was Governor of Newfoundland. It was first performed in public 21st January 1902. Both this Anthem and that for Great Britain are used.

rit.
love thee, we love thee, smil - ing land.
rit.

2. When blinding storm-gusts fret thy shore,
And wild waves lash thy strand,
Thro' sprindrift swirl and tempest roar,
We love thee, wind-swept land,
We love thee, we love thee,
We love thee, wind-swept land.

3. When spreads thy cloak of shimm'ring white,
At Winter's stern command,
Thro' shortened day and starlit night,
We love thee, frozen land,
We love thee, we love thee,
We love thee, frozen land.

4. As loved our fathers, so we love,
Where once they stood we stand,
Their prayer we raise to heav'n above,
God guard thee, Newfoundland,
God guard thee, God guard thee,
God guard thee, Newfoundland.

NEW ZEALAND
God Defend New Zealand

Words by
THOMAS BRACKEN (1843-1898)

Music by
JOHN J. WOODS (1849-1934)
Arr. by VERNON GRIFFITHS

By permission of the New Zealand Government, holders of the copyright.
This is New Zealand's National Song. The main anthem is that of Great Britain.

Thee, — God de - fend our Free - land. Guide her —
treat, God de - fend our Free - land. Guard Pa -
Thee, God de - fend our Free - land. Guide her
-na; Me A - ro - ha no - a Ki - a
— in the na - tions' van, Preach-ing love and truth to —
ci - fic's tri - ple — star From the shafts of — strife and —
in the na - tions' van, Preach-ing love — and — truth to —
hu - a ko te pai; Ki - a tau — To — a - ta —
f
Fine
man, Work - ing out Thy glo - rious plan — God de-fend New Zea - land.
war, Make her prai-ses heard a - far, God de - fend New Zea - land.
man, Work-ing out Thy glo - rious plan — God de - fend New Zea - land.
whai; Ma - na - a - ki - ti - a mai A - o - te - a - ro - a.
Fine

HIGH VOICES I (prominent)
mf
2. Men of ev - 'ry creed and race Ga - ther here be - fore Thy
HIGH VOICES II
mf
2. Men of ev - 'ry creed and race Ga - ther here be - fore Thy
LOW VOICES
mf
2. Men of ev - 'ry creed and race Ga - ther here be - fore Thy
mf
face, Ask - ing Thee to bless this place God de - fend our Free -
face, Ask - ing Thee to bless this place God de - fend our Free -
face, Ask - ing Thee to bless this place God de - fend our Free -

cresc.
land. From dis - sen-sion, en - vy, hate, And cor - rup - tion, guard our
cresc.
land. From dis - sen-sion, en - vy, hate, And cor - rup - tion, guard our
cresc.
land. From dis - sen-sion, en - vy, hate, And cor - rup - tion, guard our
cresc.
D. C. for v. 3
f
State; Make our coun-try good and great — God de - fend New Zea - land.
f
State; Make our coun-try good and great God de - fend New Zea - land.
f
State; Make our coun-try good and great — God de - fend New Zea - land.
D. C. for v. 3
f

NICARAGUA

Words by
SALOMÓN IBARRA MAYORGA
English versification by
MARY ELIZABETH SHAW

Composer unknown
(Composed before 1821)

Maestoso
Sal - ve a ti Ni - ca - ra - gua en tu
Hail Ni - ca - ra - gua! the thun - der of
sue - - lo, ya no ru - ge la
can - - non Calls thy peo - ple no
voz del can - ón ni se ti - ñe con san - gre de her-
- lon - ger to war, And thy ban - ner, twin co - loured flies

The words formerly sung were replaced by these words in 1939 by a governmental decree.

mf
- ma - - nos tu glo - rio - so pen - dón bi - co -
proud - - ly, Stained with blood of thy chil - dren no
mf
- lor, ni se ti - ñe con san - gre de her - ma - nos tu glo -
more, And thy ban - ner, twin - co - loured, flies proud - ly, Stained with
ff
ff
- rio - so pen - dón bi - co - lor. Bri - lle her -
blood of thy chil - dren no more. Gen - tle

-mo - sa la paz en tu cie - lo, na-da em - pa - ñe tu
peace spreads her wings o'er thy coun-try, Whose fair glo - ry its
glo - ria in-mor-tal que el tra - ba - jo es tu dig - no lau -
pure - ness re-tains; For thy lau - rels by la - bour are
-rel y el ho - nor es tu en-se-ña tri-un-fal,
won. Ho-nour, un-dimmed, thy shin-ing en - sign re-mains,
es tu en - se - ña tri - un - fal.
thy shin-ing en - sign re - mains.
f
f
f
f

NIGER

La Nigerienne

Words by MAURICE THIRIET

Music by
ROBERT JACQUET (b. 1896)
NICK FRIONNET (b. 1911)

Maestoso
f
dim.
p
1. Au - près du grand Ni - ger puis-sant Qui rend la na-tu-re plus bel - le,
p
So - yons fiers et re - con - nais-sants De no-tre li-ber-té nou-vel - le.
mf
E - vi - tons les vai - nes que-rel - les A - fin d'é-par - gner no-tre sang;
mf

Reproduced by permission of the composers, who hold the copyright. Niger became fully independent in 1960. This National Anthem was approved by the National Assembly of the Republic of Niger July, 1961. Words reproduced by permission of the author.

cresc.
Et que les glo - rieux ac - cents De no-tre ra - ce sans tu -
cresc.
- tel - le S'é - lèvent dans un même é - lan Jus -
f
f
- qu'à ce ciel é-blou-is - sant Où veil - le son âme é - ter -
- nel - le Qui fe - ra le pa-ys plus grand. De -
dim.
dim.

CHORUS
Allegro (2 in a bar)
mf
- bout Ni-ger: De - bout! Que no - tre œu - vre fé - conde Ra -
mf
- jeu - nis - se le cœur de ce vieux con - ti - nent Et
que ce chant s'en - tende aux qua - tre coins du mon - de Com -
- me le cri d'un Peuple é - qui - table et vail - lant! De -
f
f

-bout Ni-ger: De - bout! Sur le sol et sur l'on - de, Au
ryth - me des tam - tams, dans leur son gran - dis - sant, Res -
ff
Ped. *
-tons u-nis, tou - jours, et que cha-cun ré - pon - de A ce noble a - ve -
poco rall.
D. 𝄋 Fine
-nir qui nous dit "En a - vant."

2. *Nous retrouvons dans nos enfants*
Toutes les vertus des Ancêtres:
Pour lutter dans tous les instants
Elles sont notre raison d'être.
Nous affrontons le fauve traître
A peine armés le plus souvent
Voulant subsister dignement
Sans detruire pour nous repaître.
Dans la steppe où chacun ressent
La soif, dans le Sahel brûlant,
Marchons, sans défaillance, en maîtres
Magnanimes et vigilants.

Translation by
T.M. CARTLEDGE

1. By the waters of the mighty Niger
Which adds to the beauty of nature,
Let us be proud and grateful
For our new-won liberty.
Let us avoid vain quarrelling
So that our blood may be spared,
And may the glorious voice
Of our race, free from tutelage,
Rise unitedly, surging as from one man,
To the dazzling skies above
Where its eternal soul, watching over us,
Brings greatness to the country.

2. We find again in our children
All the virtues of our ancestors.
Such virtues are our inspiration
For fighting at every moment.
We confront ferocious and treacherous animals
Often scarcely armed,
Seeking to live in dignity,
Not slaying with a lust to kill.
In the steppe where all feel thirst,
In the burning desert,
Let us march tirelessly forward
As magnanimous and vigilant masters.

Chorus

Arise, Niger, arise! May our fruitful work
Rejuvenate the heart of this old continent,
And may this song resound around the world
Like the cry of a just and valiant people.
Arise, Niger, arise! On land and river
To the rhythm of the swelling drum-beats' sound
May we ever be united and may each one of us
Answer the call of this noble future that says to us, "Forward!"

NIGERIA

Words by
LILIAN JEAN WILLIAMS

Music by
FRANCES BENDA

Moderato
f
mp
1. Ni - ger - i - a we hail thee, Our own dear na-tive land, Though
2. Our flag shall be a sym - bol That truth and jus-tice reign, In
3. O God of all cre - a - tion, Grant this our one re - quest, Help
ff
tribe and tongue may dif - fer, In bro-ther-hood we stand, Ni -
peace or bat - tle hon - our'd, And this we count as gain, To
us to build a na - tion Where no man is op - pressed, And
-ger - ians all, and proud to serve Our sove reign Mo - ther - land.
hand on to our child - ren A ban-ner with-out stain.
so with peace and plen - ty Ni - ger - ia may be blessed.

The words and music were chosen as the result of a competition. It became the National Anthem on 1st October, 1960, when Nigeria became independent.

NORWAY

Ja, vi elsker dette landet

Words by
BJÖRNSTERNE BJÖRNSSON
(1832-1910)
Translated by
G. M. GATHORNE-HARDY

Music by
RIKARD NORDRAAK
(1842-1866)

Moderato
f
1. Ja, vi el - sker det - te lan - det,
1. Yes, we love with fond de - vo - tion
f

som det sti - ger frem, fu - ret, vær - bitt
This, the land that looms Rug - ged, storm-scarred,

o - ver van - net med de tu - sen hjem.
o'er the o - cean, With her thou - sand homes.

Adopted as the National Anthem in 1864, when first public recital was given on the fiftieth anniversary of the Norwegian constitution. Björnsson is one of Norway's great dramatists and poets.

p
Els - ker, els - ker det og ten - ker på vår far og
Love her, in our love re - call - ing Those who gave us
p
mf
cresc.
mor og den sa - ga - natt som sen - ker
birth, And old tales which night, in fall - ing,
mf
cresc.
f
ff
dröm - me på vår jord, og den sa - ga - natt som
Brings as dreams to earth, And old tales which night, in
f
ff
sen - - ker, sen - ker dröm - me på vår jord!
fall - - ing, Brings as dreams, as dreams to earth.

2. *Norske mann i hus og hytte,*
takk din store Gud!
Landet ville han beskytte,
skjönt det mörkt så ut.
Alt, hva fedrene har kjempet,
mödrene har grett,
har den Herre stille lempet,
så vi vant vår rett,
har den Herre stille lempet,
så vi vant, vi vant vår rett.

3. *Ja, vi elsker dette landet,*
som det stiger frem
furet, værbitt over vannet,
med de tusen hjem!
Og som fedres kamp har hevet
det av nöd til seir,
også vi, når det blir krevet,
for dets fred slår leir,
ogsa vi, nar det blir krevet,
for dets fred, dets fred slår leir!

2. Norseman, whatsoe'er thy station,
Thank thy God, whose power
Willed and wrought the land's salvation
In her darkest hour.
All our mothers sought with weeping
And our sires in fight,
God has fashioned, in his keeping, } *bis. (repeating* "we gained"
Till we gained our right. } *the second time)*

3. Yes, we love with fond devotion
This our land that looms
Rugged, storm-scarred, o'er the ocean
With her thousand homes.
And, as warrior sires have made her
Wealth and fame increase,
At the call we too will aid her, } *bis. (repeating* "to guard"
Armed to guard her peace. } *the second time)*

OMAN

Words by
RASHID BIN AZIZ (c.1922)

Muscat and Oman became Oman in 1970

This is sometimes played as a march. A transliterated version of the words has been approximately fitted to the music.

Translation

God save our Sultan Said;
Happy may he be with our support,
Honour and glory.
May his independence be preserved,
His banners perpetual giving their shade
Over Islam and Muslims.

PAHANG

Maestoso
mf
Ya Al - lah tu - han yang ka -
ja Pan - jang kan u - mor yang ma - ha
mu - lia ja - uh - kan da - ri pa - da Ma - ra ba -

Free Translation

Oh Almighty God,
Long live His Royal Highness!
Protect His Royal Highness from harm and danger;
Forever bless Him.

PAKISTAN

Words by
ABUL ASAR HAFEEZ JULLUNDURI

Music by
AHMAD G. CHAGLA
Arr. by BRYSON GERRARD

Music officially accepted as National Anthem of Pakistan, December 1953.
Words officially accepted as text of National Anthem of Pakistan, August 1954.

Pak sar - zamin ka ni - zam ku - wa - ti a - khu - wa - ti a -
- wam Kaum, mulk, Sul - tanat Pain - da ta bin - da bad
shad, bad man zi - li mu - rad. Par - chami si - ta - ra - o hi -
- lal Rah - ba - ri tar - ra - ki - o ka mal

Tar - ju - ma - ni ma - zi - sha - ni hal ja - ni is - tik - bal
Say - yai, khu - dai zul ja - lal.

Free Translation

1. Blessed be the sacred land,
Happy be the beauteous realm,
Symbol of high resolve,
Land of Pakistan.
Blessed be thou citadel of faith.

2. The Order of this Sacred Land
Is the might of the brotherhood of the people.
May the nation, the country, and the State
Shine in glory everlasting.
Blessed be the goal of our ambition

3. This flag of the Crescent and the Star
Leads the way to progress and perfection,
Interpreter of our past, glory of our present,
Inspiration of our future,
Symbol of Almighty's protection.

PANAMA

Himno Istmeño

Words by
JERÓNIMO de la OSSA
(1847-1907)
English versification by
SEBASTIAN SHAW

Music by
SANTOS JORGE A.
(1870-1941)
Arr. by MARTIN SHAW

Marziale

f

CHORUS
f energico

1. *Al - can - za - mos por fin — la vic - to - ria, en el cam - po fe - liz de la u - nión, Con ar - dien - tes ful - go - res de glo - ria se ilu -*

1. Fi - nal vic - to - ry honoured then our sto - ry, When at last we gained u - nion's fair field. Shin - ing bright in the blaze of her glo - ry, Now be -

f energico

This anthem was used for the first time on 4th November, 1903, when the Panamanian people carried the flag of the new Republic of Panama through the streets of the capital.

-mi - na la nue - va Na - ción
Con ar-dien-tes ful-go - res de
-hold, the new nation is re - vealed!
Shin - ing bright in the blaze of her
glo - ria se ilu - mi - na la nue - va Na - ción.
glo - ry, Now be - hold, the new nation is re - vealed!
Fine
VERSE
p dolce
Es pre - ci - so cu-brir con un ve - - lo, del pa -
We re - joice that, the Cal - va - ry end - - ed, And the
p dolce
-sa - do el cal-va - rio y la cruz,
y que a -
Cross be - ing veiled in the past,
Gen - tle

f
- dor - ne el a - zul de tu ciel - - - o, de con -
peace our blue skies has as - cend - - - ed, Down in
f
p
- cor - dia la es - plén - di - da luz. El pro -
splen - dour its ra - diance is cast. Home of
p
- gre - so a - ca - ri - cia tus la - - - res, al com -
pro - gress, and blessed by en - dea - - - vour, See, to
f
- pás de su - bli - me can - ción; ves ru -
mea - sure of mu - sic sub - lime, At your
f

-gir á tus pies am - bos ma - - - - res, que dan
feet roar two o - ceans, which se - - - - ver, For your
rum - bo a tu no - ble mi - sión.
mis - sion, a - way for all time.
D.S.

2. *En tu suelo cubierto de flores,*
A los besos del tibio terral,
Terminaron guerreros fragores,
Sólo reina el amor fraternal.
Adelante la pica y la pala,
Al trabajo sin más dilación:
Y seremos asi prez y gala
De este mundo feraz de Colón.

2. From your soil, where gay flowers are greeted
By the warmth of the breezes' caress,
Far the clamours of war have retreated;
Love fraternal your future will bless.
Then with spade and with hammer, untiring,
To his task let each man set his hand;
So, to honour and glory aspiring,
Shall we prosper Columbus' fair land.

PAPUA NEW GUINEA

O Arise All You Sons

Words and Music by
T. SHACKLADY

VERSE
(f) 1. O a - rise all you sons of this land, Let us
2. Now give thanks to the good Lord a - bove For His

sing of our joy to be free, Prais - ing God and re - joic - ing to
kind - ness, His wis - dom and love For this land of our fa - thers so

be Pa - pu - a New Gui - nea.
free, Pa - pu - a New Gui - nea.

Papua New Guinea has not yet adopted a formal National Anthem. However, "Arise all ye sons" was selected as the national song to be used at the Olympic Games in 1976. Words and music by Chief Inspector T. Shacklady, Bandmaster of the Royal Papua New Guinea Constabulary.

CHORUS

Shout our name from the moun - tains to seas - Pa - pu -
Shout a - gain for the whole world to hear - Pa - pu -

a New Gui - nea; Let us raise our voi - ces and pro -
a New Gui - nea; We're in - de - pen - dent and we're

claim Pa - pu - a New Gui - nea.
free, PA - PU - A NEW GUI - NEA.

PARAGUAY

Words by
FRANCISCO ESTEBAN ACUÑA de FIGUEROA (1791-1862)
Versified English version by
T. M. CARTLEDGE

Music transcribed by
REMBERTO GIMENEZ (b.1899)

Marciale
A los pue - blos de A - mé - ri - ca in - faus - to, Tres cen - tu - rias un ce - tro o - pri - mió, Más un dí - a so - ber - bia sur - gien - - -
Once the lands of A - me - ri - ca, sad and op-pressed, 'Neath a scep - tre for three cen - tu - ries re - mained. But one day, with their pas - sion a - ris - - -
sonoro

Adopted as National Anthem, 1846
This present arrangement was declared the official version in May 1934.
Francisco Acuña de Figueroa also wrote the words of the Uruguayan Anthem

-do, Basta!..., di - jo y el ce - - tro rom -
-ing, 'Tis e - nough! they cried and broke the pow-ers that had
-pió. Nue - stros pa - dres li -
reigned. Our fore - fa - thers, mag -
-dian - do gran - dio - - - sos, I - lus -
-ni - fi - cent - ly fight - - - ing, Showed their
-tra - ron su glo - ria mar - cial; Y tro -
mar - tial glo - ry and pow'r; And when

-za - da la augus - ta dia - de - - ma, E - nal -
they the au - gust di - a - dem had tak - - en, They joined to
-za - ron el go - rro triun - fal! Y tro -
it a cap of tri-umph in that hour, And when
-za - da la augus - ta dia - de - - ma, E - nal -
they the au - gust di - a - dem had tak - - en, They joined to
-za - ron el go - rro triun - fal. Pa - ra -
it a cap of tri-umph in that hour. Pa - ra -
CHORUS

Allegro
-gua - yos, Re-pú - bli-ca o muer - te! Nue-stro
-guay - ans, Re-pub - lic or death we choose! 'Twas our
bri - o nos dió li-ber-tad; Ni o-pre-
strength that gave us our fi-nal li-ber-ty. Nei-ther
-so - res, ni sier - vos, a-lien - tan, Don - de
ty - rants nor slaves can con-tin - ue, Where there
re-i-nan u-nión, é i-gual - dad. Ni o-pre-
reign e-qual-i-ty and u-ni - ty. Nei-ther

-so - res, ni sier - vos, a - lien - tan, Don - de
ty - rants nor slaves can con - tin - ue Where there
re - i - nan u - nión, é i - gual - dad, u - nión, é i - gual -
reign e - qual - i - ty and u - ni - ty, where reign e - qual - i -
-dad, u - nión, é i - gual - dad.
-ty, and where reign u - ni - ty.
ff

PENANG

Music by
Z. AWALUDDIN BIN Z. ALAM

Free Translation

By God's grace
Penang island is peaceful,
My noble State,
To which I owe my allegiance,
Peace and prosperity,
Progressive and successful,
The State that I love.
Unity and co-operation
For our State.

PERAK

Melody derived from an old Malay folk tune *

* This melody is also used for the National Anthem of Malaysia.

Free Translation

God bestow long life on the Sultan,
Just and prosperous shall be his reign,
Surrounded by His loyal subjects.
God bestow upon Him guidance and leadership,
God bless Perak Ridzuan,
God save the State and the Sultan.

PERLIS

Music by
ALMARHUM TUAN SYED
HAMZAR ALMARHUM SYED SAFI

Free Translation

Amen, amen – the greatest of the great,
My humble and protective prayer,
Preserve His Royal Highness and justice,
For the reign of Jamalullail.

The melody, composed in 1930, was harmonised by Raymond G. Isles.

PERU

Words by
JOSÉ DE LA TORRE UGARTE
(1786-1831)

Music by
JOSÉ BERNARDO ALCEDO (1788-1878)
Arr. by HENRY COLEMAN

Words and music chosen as result of a competition for a national anthem promoted by General San Martin in 1821.
They were declared official on 12th February, 1913.

-te - mos al vo - to so - lem - ne que la Pa - tria al E - ter-no e-le -
-vó ___ que fal - te - mos al vo - to so - lem - ne que ___ la
Pa - tria al E - ter - no e-le - vó ___ que fal - te - mos al vo - to so -
-lem - ne que ___ la Pa - tria al E - ter - no e-le - vó. ___
f
ff
Fine

VERSE
p
1. Lar - go tiem - po el pe - rua - no o - pri - mi - - do la o - mi -
p
- no - sa ca - de - na arras - tró; con - de - na - do a u - na cruel ser - vi -
cresc.
cresc.
f
p
- dum - - bre, lar - go tiem - po lar - go tiem - po lar - go
f
p
tiem - po en si - len - cio gi - mió. Mas a - pe - nas el gri - to sa -
p
p

-gra-do ¡Li-ber-tad! en sus cos-tas___ se o-yó, la in-do-
p
-len-cia de es-cla-vo sa-cu-de, la hu-mi-lla-do la hu-mi-
p
f
-lla-do la hu-mi-lla-do cerviz le-van-tó,___ la hu-mi-
f
p
rall. molto
a tempo
f
D.S.
-lla-do cer-viz le-van-tó cer-viz le-van-tó.___ So-mos
D.S.
p
rall. molto
f a tempo
3
3

Free Translation

CHORUS

We are free; let us always be so,
and let the sun rather deny its light
than that we should fail the solemn vow
which our Country raised to God.

VERSE

For a long time the Peruvian, oppressed,
dragged the ominous chain;
condemned to cruel serfdom,
for a long time he moaned in silence.
But as soon as the sacred cry of
Freedom! was heard on his coasts
he shakes the indolence of the slave,
he raises his humiliated head.

NOTE: There were originally six verses, but this first verse only is now sung.

THE PHILIPPINES

Original Spanish words by
JOSÉ PALMA (1876-1903)
New Tagalog translation by
FELIPE P. DE LEON.
English trans. by M.A.L. Lane

Music by
JULIAN FELIPE (1861-1944)

Alla marcia
Tagalog. Ba - yang ma - gi - liw, Per-las ng Si - la - nga - ñan,
Land of the morn - ing, Child of the sun re - turn - ing,
A - lab ng pu - so Sa dib-dib mo'y bu - hay.
With fer - vour burn - ing Thee do our souls a - dore.
Lu - pang hi - ni - rang, Du - yan ka ng ma - gi - ting,
Land dear and ho - ly, Cra - dle of no - ble he - roes,

First performed in conjunction with the reading of the Act of Proclamation of Philippine Independence, 12 June 1898. The words were written in 1899.

Fine
Sa man - lu - lu - pig Di ka pa - si - si - il.
Ne'er shall in - va - ders Tram-ple thy sa - cred shore.
Fine
Sa da - gat at bun - dok, Sa si - moy at sa
Ev - er with - in thy skies and through thy clouds And
la - ngit mong bug - haw, May di - lag ang tu - la At
o'er thy hills and sea Do we be - hold the ra - diance,
a - wit sa pag - la - yang mi - na - ma -
Feel the throb, Of glo - rious lib - er -

-hal. Ang kis-lap ng wa-ta-wat mo'y Ta-gum-pay
-ty. Thy ban-ner, dear to all our hearts, Its
na nag-ni-ning-ning; Ang bi-tu-in at a-raw
sun and stars a-light, O nev-er shall its
niya, Kai-lan pa ma'y di mag-di-di-lim,
shin-ing field Be dim-med by ty-rant's might.
Fine
ff
Lu-pà ng A-raw, ng lu-wal-ha-ti't pag-sin-ta Bu-hay ay
Beau-ti-ful land of love, O land of light, In thine em-

la - ngit sa pi - ling mo; A-ming li -
-brace 'tis rap - ture to lie; But it is
-ga - ya, na pag ma'y mang - a - a - pi, Ang ma-ma -
glo - ry ev - er, When thou art wronged For us, thy
-tay nang da - hil sa - iyo.
sons, to suf - fer and die.
D.C. al Fine
D.C. al Fine
Ped.
*

THE PHILIPPINES

Original words written in Spanish

Tierra adorada.
hija del sol de Oriente
su fuego ardiente
en ti latiendo esta.

Tierra de amores,
del heroismo cuna,
los invasores
no te hollaran jamas.

En tu azul cielo, en tus auras,
en tus montes y en tu mar
esplende y late el poema
de tu amada libertad.

Tu pabellon que en las lides
la victoria ilumino
no veranunca apagados
sus estrellas ni su sol.

Tierra de dichas, de sol y amores,
en tu regazo dulce es vivir;
es una gloria para tus hijos,
cuando te ofenden, por ti morir.

POLAND

Words by
General JÓZEF WYBICKI
(1747-1822)
Translated by
MARTIN SHAW

Music: Traditional

Allegretto vivace

f

Jeszc - ze Pol - ska nie zgi-nę - ta, kie - dy my zy - je - my, co nam ob - ca prze - moc wzię - ta, szab-lą od - bie - rze - my. Marsz, marsz, Dą - brow - ski;

Po - land still is ours for ev - er, Long as Poles re - main; Chains the foe bound on her nev - er Shall the foe re - tain. On! On! Da - bru - ski!★ from

f *mf* *mf*

This song, first sung in 1795, was a favourite with the Polish Legions in the Napoleonic wars. It has been sung all over Poland since 1912; in 1927 it was authorized as its National Anthem by the new Polish republican government.

★General Dabruski (1755-1818) commanded the Polish Legions. General Wybicki was among those who organised and led the Legions. He was also a poet and a member of the Polish Parliament.

cresc.
z zie mi włoskiej do Polski!
I-ta-ly's fair plain!
f
Za twoim prze-
Lead us on to
cresc.
f
-wodem złaczym się z narodem.
greet our home-land, Lead us back a-gain!

2. *Przejdziem Wisłę, przejdziem Wartę,*
będziem Polakami,
dał nam przykład Bonaparte
jak zwyciężać mamy.
Marsz, marsz, Dąbrowski

2. Vistula and Wartar over,
Poles we'll ever be;
And from Bonaparte discover
Paths to victory.
On! On! etc.

3. *Jak Czarniecki do Poznania*
po szwedzkim zaborze,
dla ojczyzny ratowania
wrócim się przez morze.
Marsz, marsz, Dąbrowski

3. When the Swede had forged our chain,
The Fatherland to save,
Czarniecki, Poznan town to gain,
Plunged into the wave.
On! On! etc.

PORTUGAL

Words by
HENRIQUE LOPES DE MENDONÇA (1856-1931)

Music by
ALFREDO KEIL
(1850-1907)
Arr. by HENRY COLEMAN

Grandioso
mf
f
mf
1. Herois do mar, no - bre
po - vo, Na-ção va-len - - te, i-mor-tal, Le-van-
-tai ho - je de no - - vo O es-plen-dor de Por-tu-
gal! En - tre as bru - mas da me-mó - ria, Ó
p
p

First played January 1890, approved as the National Anthem in 1910.

Pá - tria, sen - te - se a voz
Dos teus e - gré - gios a -
vós,
Que há - de gui - ar - te à vi - tó - ri - a!
f
Às
ar - mas! Às ar - mas!
mf
So - bre a ter - ra, so - bre o
mar
CHORUS
f
Às ar - mas! Às ar - mas!
cresc.
Pe - la
3

ff
Pá - tria lu - tar! Con-tra os ca-nhões mar-char, mar-char!
ff

2. *Desfralda a invicta bandeira*
À luz viva do teu céu!
Brade à Europa à terra inteira:
Portugal não pereceu!
Beija o solo teu jucundo
O Oceano a rugir d'amor;
E o teu braço vencedor
Deu novos mundos ao mundo!

Às armas, às armas!
Sobre a terra, sobre o mar,
Às armas, às armas!
Pela pátria lutar!
Contra os canhões marchar,
Marchar!

3. *Saudai o sol que desponta*
Sobre um ridente porvir;
Seja o eco de uma afronta
O sinal do ressurgir.
Ráios dessa aurora forte
São como beijos de mãe
Que nos guardam, nos sustêm
Contra as injúrias da sorte.

Às armas, às armas!
Sobre a terra, sobre o mar,
Às armas, às armas!
Pela pátria lutar!
Contra os canhões marchar,
Marchar!

1. Heroes of the sea, noble race
valiant and immortal nation,
now is the hour to raise up on high once more
Portugal's splendour.
From out of the mists of memory,
oh Homeland, we hear the voices
of your great forefathers
that shall lead you on to victory!

CHORUS

To arms, to arms
on land and sea!
To arms, to arms
to fight for our Homeland!
To march against the enemy guns!

2. Unfurl the unconquerable flag
in the bright light of your sky!
Cry out to all Europe and the whole world
that Portugal has not perished.
Your happy land is kissed
by the Ocean that murmurs with love.
And your conquering arm
has given new worlds to the world!

CHORUS

To arms, to arms
on land and sea!
To arms, to arms
to fight for our Homeland!
To march against the enemy guns!

3. Salute the Sun that rises
on a smiling future:
let the echo of an insult be
the signal for our revival.
The rays of that powerful dawn
are like a mother's kisses
that protect us and support us
against the insults of fate.

CHORUS

To arms, to arms
on land and sea!
To arms, to arms
to fight for our Homeland!
To march against the enemy guns!

PUERTO RICO

La Borinqueña

No words

Music by F. ASTOL
Arranged by RAMÓN COLLADO

This anthem was designated as the Anthem of Puerto Rico in 1952. It has no official words. Its use is governed by a Regulation promulgated by the Secretary of State of Puerto Rico on May 2nd 1960, according to Act Nº 2 of the Legislative Assembly of 24th July 1952. The Puerto Ricans, being American citizens, also use the anthem of the U.S.A.

QATAR

RHODESIA

LUDWIG VAN BEETHOVEN (1770-1827)
Arr. by K. R. MACDONALD

(f)
1. Rise, O voi - ces of Rho - de - sia.
2. Rise, O voi - ces of Rho - de - sia,
(f)
God, may we Thy boun - ty share.
bring - ing her your proud ac - claim,
Give us strength to face all dan - ger
Grand - ly ech - oing through the moun - tains,

In August 1974 the choral theme of the last movement of Beethoven's ninth symphony was selected to be the National Anthem of Rhodesia, and first played at the opening of Parliament in Salisbury on 27 August 1974. The words were added later.

An arrangement by Herbert von Karajan of this music is the official anthem for the Council of Europe.

and, where chal - lenge is, to dare; Guide us, Lord, to
rol - ling o - ver far - flung plain, Roar - ing in the
wise de - ci - sion, e - ver of Thy grace a - ware. Oh,
might - y ri - vers, join - ing in one grand re - frain, As -
let our hearts beat brave - ly al - ways for this land with - in Thy care.
cend - ing to the sun - lit hea - vens, tel - ling of her hon - oured name.

ROMANIA

Trăiască Regele

Words by
VASILE ALECSANDRI

Music by
EDWARD A. HÜBSCH (1813-1894)
Arr. by HENRY COLEMAN

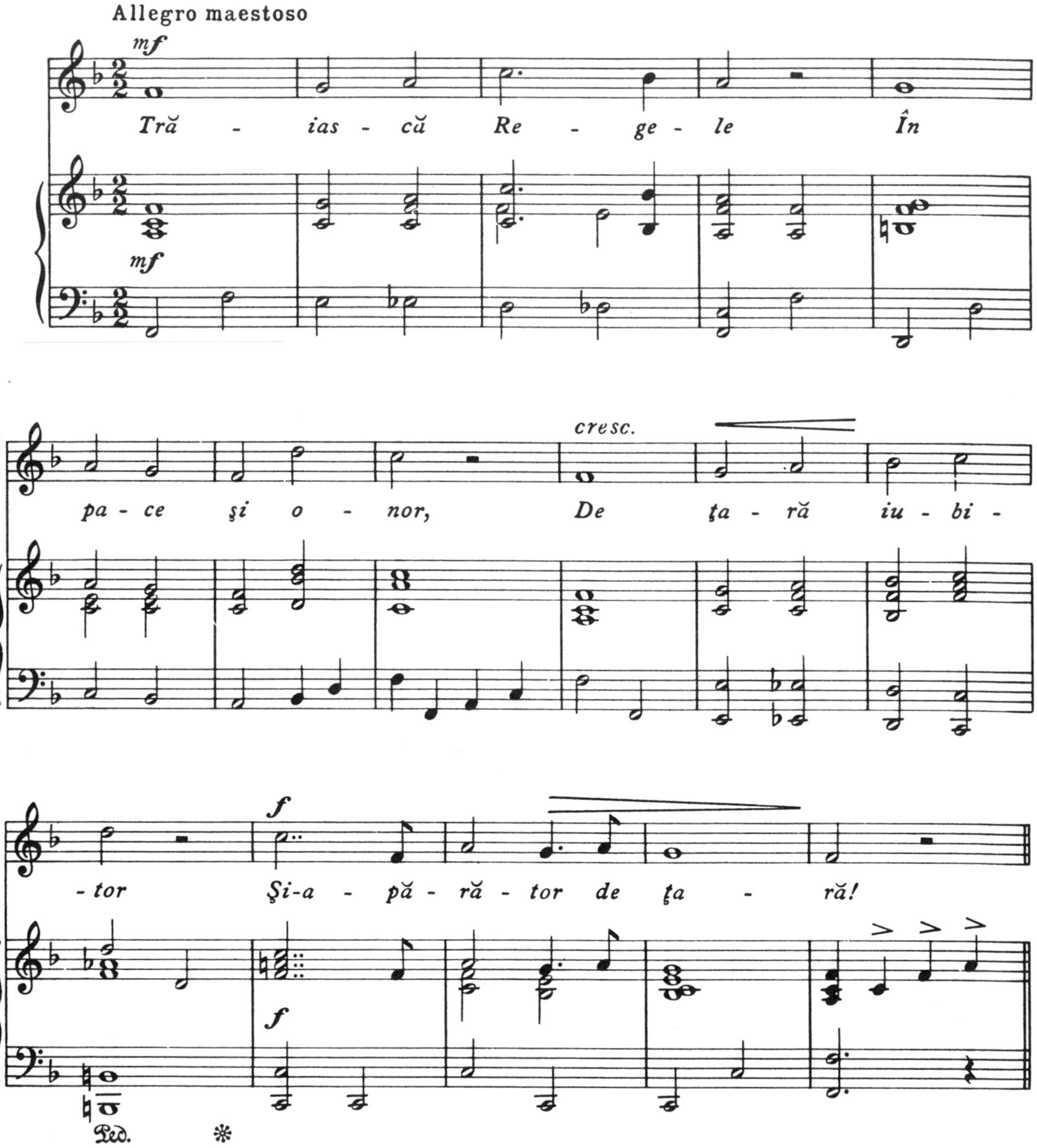

Allegro maestoso

mf

Tră - ias - că Re - ge - le În

mf

cresc.

pa - ce şi o - nor, De ţa - ră iu - bi -

f
- tor Şi-a - pă - ră - tor de ţa - ră!
f
Ped.

This National Anthem of Romania (which was proclaimed a kingdom on 10th May, 1881) is at present not sung inside Romania as the anthem which follows has officially replaced it.

f risoluto
Fi - e Domn glo - ri - os Pes - te -
f sempre
- noi, Fi - e'n veci no - ro -
- cos În răz - boi!
rall.
ff meno mosso
O! Doam - ne Sfin - te, Ce - resc Pă -

2. *Traiască Patria*
Cât soarele ceresc,
Rai dulce, românesc,
Ce poartă-un mare nume!
Fie'n veci el ferit
De nevoi!
Fie'n veci locuit
De eroi!
O! Doamne Sfinte,
Ceresc Părinte
Întinde-a ta mână
Pe țara română!

1. Long live our King
In peace and honour,
Loving his country
Defending our fatherland!
Let him be glorious
Rule over us,
Always victorious
In war.
O Lord the Holy,
Our heavenly Father,
Support with thy hands
The Romanian Crown!

2. Long live our fatherland
As long as the sun,
Sweet paradise
With glorious name!
Let it always be free
Of worries!
Let it always be inhabited
By heroes!
O Lord the Holy
Our heavenly Father,
Protect with thy hand
The Romanian land!

Pronunciation:

ă like er in "father"
Î like u in "une" in French
e (throughout) as in "get"
ț as ts
ce as che
Şi-a as sha
veci as vech
ge as in gentle

ROMANIA

No words

Music by
MATEI SOCOR
(b. 1908)

ff *mf* *mf*

This officially became the National Anthem in 1953.
Words were originally used but these were abolished in 1964

f
ff
mf
ff
Ped.
Ped.
Ped.

RWANDA

Rwanda rwacu

This anthem was adopted by the National Assembly and sanctioned by the President of the Republic on 11th December 1962, the year when Rwanda became independent.

nshi - mi - ra A-ba-rwa - na - shya - ka ba-za - nye Re - pu - bu - li - ka
Shi - ng'u - mu-zi De-mo - ka - ra - si wa-du - ha - ye kwi-to - re-ra
Ga - tu - tsi, Ga-twa na ga - hu - tu na-mwe ba - nya-rwa-nda ba-ndi
I - nte - go ya-cu Ba - nya - rwa - nda twi-shyi - re ka-ndi twi-za - ne
ff
i - da-hi-nyu-ka. Ba-va-ndi-mwe b'u - ru Rwa-nda
a - ba-te-ge-tsi. Ba-nya-rwa-nda: a - ba-ku-ru
mwa - byi - ye-me-je, I-nde-pa-nda-nsi twa-tsi-ndi-ye
mu Rwa-nda rwa-cu. Twe-se ha-mwe, twu-ng'u-bu-mwe
ff
ff
f
rwa-cu twe-se ni - mu-ha-gu-ru-ke: Tu - ru-bu-mba-ti-re mu ma -
na-mw'a-ba-to mwi-zi-hi-y'u Rwa-nda: Tu - ru-bu-mba-ti-re mu ma -
twe-se ha-mwe tu - yi-shyi-gi-ki-re: Tu - yi-bu-mba-ti-re mu ma -
nta mu-su-su du - te - r'i-mbe-re ko: Tu - ru-bu-mba-ti-re mu ma -
f

molto rit.
- ho - ro, mu ku - li, mu bwi - ge - nge no mu bwu - mvi - ka - ne.
- ho - ro, mu ku - li, mu bwi - ge - nge no mu bwu - mvi - ka - ne.
- ho - ro, mu ku - li, mu bwi - ge - nge no mu bwu - mvi - ka - ne.
- ho - ro, mu ku - li, mu bwi - ge - nge no mu bwu - mvi - ka - ne.
molto rit.

1. My Rwanda, land that gave me birth,
Fearlessly, tirelessly, I boast of you!
When I recall your achievements to this very day,
I praise the pioneers who have brought in our unshakeable Republic.
Brothers all, sons of this Rwanda of ours,
Come rise up all of you,
Let us cherish her in peace and in truth,
In freedom and in harmony!

2. Let the victory drums beat throughout all Rwanda!
The Republic has swept away feudal bondage.
Colonialism has faded away like a worn-out shoe.
Democracy take root!
Through you we have chosen our own rulers.
People of Rwanda, old and young, citizens all,
Let us cherish her in peace and in truth,
In freedom and in harmony!

3. Home-born Rwandans all, beat the victory drums!
Democracy has triumphed in our land.
All of us together we have striven for it arduously.
Together we have decreed it– Tutsi, Twa, Hutu, with other racial elements,
This hard-won Independence of ours,
Let us all join to build it up!
Let us cherish it in peace and in truth,
In freedom and in harmony!

4. Come let us extol our Flag!
Long live our President, long live the citizens of our land!
Let this be our aim, people of Rwanda:
To stand on our own feet, in our own right, by our own means.
Let us promote unity and banish fear.
Let us go forward together in Rwanda.
Let us cherish her in peace and in truth,
In freedom and in harmony!

SABAH

Words and Music by
H.B. HERMANN

Moderato
Sa - bah ta - nah ay-er ku, Ne-ge-
Sa - bah my mo - ther - land, Our
ri ki-ta yang ter-chin - ta, Pe-mu - da, Pe-mu-di se-mu-
most be - loved home - land, Come all young men and
a ma-ri lah Ba-ngun lah ber-sa-tu se-mu - a, Ma-ri
wo - men a-rise, Let us all u - nite to - ge - - ther. Come

lah ber - sa - ma ser - ta ma - ju ja - ya Mer - de -
all! U - nite and work to - ge - ther For
ka sa-pan-jang ma - sa, Ber-sa - tu se-ga-la bang -
Free-dom for ev - er and ev - - er. To - ge - ther let all peo-ple
ff rall.
sa sen-to-sa Sa - bah Ne-gri Mer - de - ka!
strive For the peace and free - dom of Sa - bah!
ff rall.

SAINT LUCIA

Words by
FATHER C. JESSE

Music by
LEYTON THOMAS
Arr. by W. L. REED

(♩ = 110)
p
Sons and daugh-ters of St. Lu-cia, Love the land that gave us birth,
Gone the times when na-tions bat-tled For this 'He-len of the West',
May the good Lord bless our is-land, Guard her sons from woe and harm!
f cresc.
rit.
Land of bea-ches, hills and val-leys, Fair-est isle of all the earth.
Gone the days when strife and dis-cord Dimmed her chil-dren's toil and rest.
May our peo-ple live u-ni-ted, Strong in soul and strong in arm.
cresc.
f rall.
Where-so-ev-er you may roam Love, oh love your is-land home!
Dawns at last a brigh-ter day, Stret-ches out a glad new way.
Jus-tice, Truth and Cha-ri-ty, Our i-deal for e-ver be!

Adopted on achieving statehood 5 March 1967

SAN MARINO

Words by
GIOSUÈ CARDUCCI
(1835-1907)

Music by
FEDERICO CONSOLO
(1841-1906)

Largo solemno
ff
O - no - re a te o - no - re o an - ti - ca Re -
ff
- pu - bli - ca vir - tuo - - - sa - tuo - - - sa
pp
- ge - ne - ro - - - sa fi - den - te o - no - re a
pp

Free Translation

Honour to you, O ancient Republic,
Virtuous, generous, faithful!
Honour to you, and live eternally
Within the life and the glory of Italy.

SARAWAK

Arranged by
W. L. REED

(♩= 118)
mf
Sa - ra - wak ne - gri ku ber - dau - lat mer - de - ka Rak - yat
nya hi - dup te - guh ber - sa - tu pa - du. Se - mua ber - a - zam
te - rus ber - khid Mat pa - da ne - ga - ra.

Free Translation

Sarawak, my free and sovereign State,
The people dwell in unity.
We all aspire to serve the State.

God bless the State and may it grow,
Firm in its people's love and faith,
A faith that calls for life itself.
Pray she remains forever in the heart of Malaysia.

SAUDI ARABIA

Words by
MUHAMMAD TALAAT

Music by
ABDUR REHMAN ALKHATIB

First performed 1947, adopted 1950.

YA EESHO MALIKONAL-HABEEB
HAY-YAH TIFOO
HAY-YAH-FA-OO
IHTIFOO WARADDIDON-NASHEED

ARWAHONA FIDAHO HA-MIL HARAM
AASHAL-MALIK
RAYATAL-WATTAN
YA EESHO YA EESHO YA EESHOUL-MALIK

Unofficial Translation

Long live our glorious King
To him raise applause.
Applaud, and repeat the song
we raise to the Protector
Of the Holy Land
Long live the King
And the flag of the country
Long live the King!

SELANGOR

Music by
ENCIK SAIFUL BAHRI

Maestoso
mf
Du - li yang ma - ha mu - li - a Se -
mf
la - mat di - a - tas takh - ta Al -
lah lan - jut - kan u - sia tu - an - ku Ra -

Anthem adopted on 8 March, 1967.

Free Translation

His Royal Highness,
Safe on the throne,
By God's grace long live His Royal Highness.
Subjects offer their blessings
To His Royal Highness.
Bless His Royal Highness forever;
Peace and security
For His Royal Highness.

SENEGAL

Words by
LEOPOLD SÉDAR SENGHOR (b.1906)
Music by
HERBERT PEPPER
KORA* Cadenza
Alla Marcia
1. Pin-cez tous vos Ko-ras, Frap-pez les ba-la-fons, Le
Lion rouge a ru-gi Le Domp-teur de la brousse d'un
bond s'est é-lan-cé Dis-si-pant les tén-è-bres. So-

Senegal became independent on 4th April 1960
This National Anthem was adopted in 1960
The words are by the President, Leopold Sédar Senghor

*Harp-Lute of the Senegalese Griots.

-leil sur nos ter-reurs, So - leil sur nos es-poirs.
De-bout frè - res voi - ci l'A-fri-que ras-sem-blé - e.
3
CHORUS
Fi - bres de mon coeur vert, E-pau-le contre é-pau-le,
Mes plus que frères O Sé - né-ga-lais, de-bout!

2. *Sénégal, toi le fils de l'écume du Lion,*
Toi surgi de la nuit au galop des chevaux,
Rends-nous, oh! rends-nous l'honneur de nos Ancêtres,
Splendides comme ébène et forts comme le muscle
Nous disons droits– l'épée n'a pas une bavure.

3. *Sénégal, nous faisons nôtre ton grand dessein:*
Rassembler les poussins à l'abri des milans
Pour en faire, de l'Est à l'Ouest, du Nord au Sud,
Dressé, un même peuple, un peuple sans couture
Mais un peuple tourné vers tous les vents du monde.

4. *Sénégal, comme toi, comme tous nos héros,*
Nous serons durs sans haine et des deux bras ouverts.
L'épée, nous la mettrons dans la paix du fourreau,
Car le travail sera notre arme et la parole.
Le Bantou est un frère, et l'Arabe et le Blanc.

5. *Mais que si l'ennemi incendie nos frontières*
Nous serons tous dressés et les armes au poing:
Un Peuple dans sa foi défiant tous les malheurs,
Les jeunes et les vieux, les hommes et les femmes.
La Mort, oui! Nous disons la Mort, mais pas la honte.

Free Translation by
ELIZABETH P. COLEMAN

1. Sound, all of you, your Koras,
Beat the drums,
The red Lion has roared,
The Tamer of the bush with one leap has rushed forward
Scattering the gloom.
Light on our terrors,
Light on our hopes.
Arise, brothers, Africa behold united.

Chorus

Shoulder to shoulder,
O people of Senegal, more than brothers to me, arise!
Unite the sea and the springs,
Unite the steppe and the forest.
Hail, mother Africa,
Hail, mother Africa.

2. Senegal, thou son of the Lion,
Arise in the night with great speed,
Restore, oh, restore to us the honour of our ancestors,
Magnificent as ebony and strong as muscles,
We are a straight people—the sword has no fault.

3. Senegal, we make your great design our own:
To gather the chicks, sheltering them from kites,
To make from them, from East to West, from North to South,
A people rising as one, in seamless unity,
Yet a people facing all the winds of the earth.

4. Senegal, like thee, like all our heroes,
We will be stern without hatred, and with open arms.
The sword we will put peacefully in its sheath,
For work and words will be our weapon.
The Bantu is our brother, the Arab, and the White man too.

5. But if the enemy violates our frontiers,
We will all be ready, weapons in our hands;
A people in its faith defying all evil;
Young and old, men and women,
Death, yes! but not dishonour.

SIERRA LEONE

Words by
C. N. FYLE

Music by JOHN J. AKAR
Arr. by HENRY COLEMAN

Maestoso

f

1. High we ex-alt__ thee, realm of the free; Great is the love__ we have for__ thee; Firm-ly u-nit-ed e-ver we stand, Sing-ing thy praise, O__ nat-ive__ land. We raise up our hearts and our

p

Written and composed in 1961 and adopted as the National Anthem when Sierra Leone achieved independence on 27th April 1961
Both author and composer are Sierra Leonians; C.N. Fyle being a tutor at a boys' high school, and John J. Akar Director of the Sierre Leone Broadcasting Service.

cresc.
voic - es on high, the hills and the val-leys re - e - cho our cry;
cresc.
ff
Bless-ing and peace be e-ver thine own, Land that we love, our_ Sier-ra Le-one.
ff
rall.

2. One with a faith that wisdom inspires,
One with a zeal that never tires;
Ever we seek to honour thy name,
Ours is the labour, thine the fame.
We pray that no harm on thy children may fall,
That blessing and peace may descend on us all;
So may we serve thee ever alone,
Land that we love, our Sierra Leone.

3. Knowledge and truth our forefathers spread,
Mighty the nations whom they led;
Mighty they made thee, so too may we
Show forth the good that is ever in thee.
We pledge our devotion, our strength and our might,
Thy cause to defend and to stand for thy right;
All that we have be ever thine own,
Land that we love, our Sierra Leone.

SINGAPORE
Majulah Singapura

Words and Music by
ZUBIR SAID (b. 1907)
Arr. by HENRY COLEMAN

For Royal Salute play from ★ to ★

First performed September, 1958. It became very popular and when Singapore became self-governing on 3rd June 1959 it was decided to make it the National Anthem. It was officially adopted as such by the Legislative Assembly of Singapore on 30th November, 1959.

Free Translation

Let us, the people of Singapore, together march forward towards happiness. Our noble aspiration is to see Singapore achieve success.
Let us unite in a new spirit. We all pray:
"May Singapore Progress", "May Singapore Progress".

SOMALIA

No words

Music, traditional.
Transcribed by R.A.Y. MITCHELL
Piano arr. by HENRY COLEMAN

This traditional music was adopted as the National Anthem when Somaliland became independent on 26 June, 1960. It was recorded by village musicians and transcribed by R.A.Y. Mitchell, Bandmaster of the Military Band of The Royal Highland Fusiliers, who performed it at Independence Celebrations

SOUTH AFRICA

Die Stem van Suid-Afrika

THE CALL OF SOUTH AFRICA

Words by
C.J. LANGENHOVEN, (1873-1932)
Official English translation, 1952, amended 1959

Music by
M.L. de VILLIERS
(b. 1885)

Alla marcia
mf
1. Uit die blou van on se he - mel, uit die diep - te van ons see,
2. In die merg van ons ge - been - te, in ons hart en siel en gees,
1. Ring-ing out from our blue hea - vens, from our deep seas break-ing round;
2. In our bo - dy and our spi - rit, in our in - most heart held fast;
mf
Oor ons e - wi - ge ge - berg - tes waar die
In ons roem op ons ver - le - de, in ons
O - ver e - ver - last - ing moun - tains where the
In the prom - ise of our fu - ture and the

Adopted in 1936; English version adopted in 1952, revised 1959.

with emphasis
kran - se— ant - woord gee, Deur ons vér ver - la - te
hoop op— wat sal wees, In ons wil en werk en
e - choing crags re - sound; From our plains where creak - ing
glo - ry— of our past; In our will, our work, our
a tempo
vlak - tes met die kreun van os - se - wa— Ruis die
wan - del, van ons wieg tot aan ons graf— Deel geen
wag - ons cut their trails in - to the earth— Calls the
striv - ing, from the cra - dle to the grave— There's no
stem van ons ge - lief - de, van ons land Suid - A - fri -
an - der land ons lief - de, trek geen an - der— trou ons
spi - rit of our Coun - try, of the land that— gave us
land that shares our lov - ing, and no bond that— can en -

f with enthusiasm
dim.
-ka. Ons sal ant-woord op jou roep-stem, ons sal
af. Va-der-land! ons sal die a-del van jou
birth. At thy call we shall not fal-ter, firm and
-slave. Thou hast borne us and we know thee. May our
f
dim.
earnestly
cresc.
triumphantly
of-fer wat jy vra: Ons sal le-we, ons sal
naam met e-re dra: Waar en trou as A-fri-
stead-fast we shall stand, At thy will to live or
deeds to all pro-claim Our en-dur-ing love and
cresc.
ff
ster-we- ons vir jou, Suid-A-fri-ka.
-ka-ners- kin-ders van Suid-A-fri-ka.
per-ish, O South A-fri-ca, dear land.
ser-vice to thy hon-our and thy name.
ff

3 *In die songloed van ons somer, in ons winternag se kou,*
In die lente van ons liefde, in die lanfer van ons rou,
By die klink van huw'liks-klokkies, by die kluitklap op die kis—
Streel jou stem ons nooit verniet nie, weet jy waar jou kinders is.
Op jou roep sê ons nooit nee nie, sê ons altyd, altyd ja;
Om te lewe, on te sterwe-ja, ons kom, Suid-Afrika.

4 *Op U Almag vas vertrouend het ons vadere gebou:*
Skenk ook ons die krag, o Here! om te handhaaf en te hou—
Dat die erwe van ons vaad're vir ons kinders erwe bly:
Knegte van die Allerhoogste, teen die hele wêreld vry.
Soos ons vadere vertrou het, leer ook ons vertrou, o Heer—
Met ons land en met ons nasie sal dit wel wees, God regeer.

3 In the golden warmth of summer, in the chill of winter's air,
In the surging life of springtime, in the autumn of despair;
When the wedding bells are chiming or when those we love depart,
Thou dost know us for thy children and dost take us to thy heart.
Loudly peals the answering chorus: We are thine, and we shall stand,
Be it life or death, to answer to thy call, beloved land.

4 In thy power, Almighty, trusting, did our fathers build of old;
Strengthen then, O Lord, their children to defend, to love, to hold—
That the heritage they gave us for our children yet may be:
Bondsmen only to the Highest and before the whole world free.
As our fathers trusted humbly, teach us, Lord, to trust Thee still:
Guard our land and guide our people in Thy way to do Thy will.

SPAIN
MARCHA REAL

No words

18th-Century tune
Orchestrated by
BARTOLOMÉ PÉREZ CASAS (b.1873)
Arr. by MARTIN SHAW

This anthem, the *Marcha Real*, dates from 3rd September, 1770, when it was declared by Royal Decree of Carlos III as the Spanish Royal March. In July 1942 General Franco issued a decree declaring it as the national hymn. There are no official words, though various writers have written verses at different times.

SRI LANKA
(CEYLON)
Sri Lankā Māthā

Words and melody by
ANANDA SAMARAKOON
Arr. by SURYA SENA

Sri Lanka is the official name for Ceylon which became a Republic on 22 May 1973. The first two words were changed.

ni, Su-rän-di a-thi So - ba-mā - na Lan - kā
Ped. * Ped. * Ped. *
Dhan - ya dhan-a - ya ne - ka mal pa - la thu - ru pi - ri,
ja-ya bhoom - i - ya ram - yā. A-pa ha-ta sä-pa si-ri
p
p
se-tha sad-a-nā, jee - va-na-yē Mā - thā!

mf
Pi-li-ga-nu ma-na a-pa bhak-ti poo-ja, Na-mō Na-mō Mā-
mf
thā. A-pa Sri Lan-kā, Na-mō Na-
f
f
mō Na-mō Na-mō Mā-thā, a-pa Sri Lan-
ff
ff
kā, Na-mō Na-mō Na-mō Na-mō Mā-thā.
Ped.

2. *Obave apa vidya obamaya apa sathya*
..... obave apa shakti
apa hada thula bhakti oba apa āloke
apage anuprane oba apa jeevana ve
apa muktiya obave

3. *Nava jēēvana demine nithina apa*
pubudu karan māthā
Gnana vēērya vadavamina ragena yanu
mana jaya bhōōmi karā
Eka mavekuge daru kala bavinā
yamu yamu wee nopamā
Prema vadamu sama bheda durara
Namō Namō Māthā

Free Translation by Dr. C.W.W. Kannangara

Mother Lanka– we worship Thee!
Plenteous in prosperity, Thou,
Beauteous in grace and love,
Laden with corn and luscious fruit
And fragrant flowers of radiant hue,
Giver of life and all good things,
Our land of joy and victory,
Receive our grateful praise sublime,
Lanka! we worship Thee.

Thou gavest us Knowledge and Truth,
Thou art our strength and inward faith,
Our light divine and sentient being,
Breath of life and liberation.
Grant us, bondage free, inspiration.
Inspire us for ever.
In wisdom and strength renewed,
Ill-will, hatred, strife all ended,
In love enfolded, a mighty nation
Marching onward, all as one,
Lead us, Mother, to fullest freedom.

SUDAN

Words by
AHMED MOHAMED SALIH
English versification by
T. M. CARTLEDGE

Music by
ARCHMED MURGAN
Arr. by T. M. CARTLEDGE

Moderato
NAḤ-NU DJUN-DUL-LÂH DJUN-DUL-WA-TAN.
We are the ar-my of God and of our land,
IN DÄ Â DÂ ʿIL FI-DÂ LÄM NA-KhUN.
We shall ne-ver fail, called to make sac-ri-fice.
NÄ-TÄ-HAD-DAL MAUT ʿEND-ÄL-MI-ḤAN.
Wheth-er brav-ing death, hard-ship or pain,

f
NÄSh - TÄ RIL — MÄDJD BI ÄGh - LÂ - ThÄ-MÄN.
We for glo - ry give our lives as the price.
f
HÂ - ThI-HIL ARD LÄ-NÂ! FÄL - YÄ-'ISh SÛ - DÂ - NU-NÂ,
This our land, our Su-dan, Long may she now live, we pray,
'A - LA-MAN BÄYN ÄL U - MÄM.
Show-ing all na - tions the way.

YÄ BE-NIS - SÛ - DÂN,
Sons of the Su - dan,
HÄ - ThÄRAM - ZU-KUM:
sum - moned now to serve.

YAḤ MI - LUL - ʻEB, WÄ YAḤ - MÎ AR - DA - KUM.
Shoul - der - ing the task our coun - try to pre - serve.

Key to phonetic transliteration of Arabic text

^ for long vowels

Û as *oo* in *pool*

U nearer *u* in *put*

Ä as *a* in *cat*

A as *a* in *rather*

ÄYN approx. as *ine* in *fine*

Th ① as *th* in *thing*

Th ② as *th* in *this*

Ḥ aspirated at back of mouth

Kh like hard *ch* in German *Buch*

Gh like gutteral *r* in French *rang*

ʻ like last *a* of *China*

AUT like *out*

SURINAM

Words by
C. A. HOEKSTRA (1893)

Music by
C. de PUY (1876)
Arr. by HENRY COLEMAN

Moderato
f
God zij met ons Su - ri - na - me! Hij ver-
O - po kon - dre - man oen o - po Sra - nan-
f
-heff' ons heer - lijk land! Hoe wij hier ook sa - men
-gron e ka - ri oen. Wans o - pe ta - ta ko -
kwa - men, aan zijn grond zijn wij ver - pand. Wer-kend
- mo - po, wi moe se - ti kon - dré boen. Stré de
mf
mf

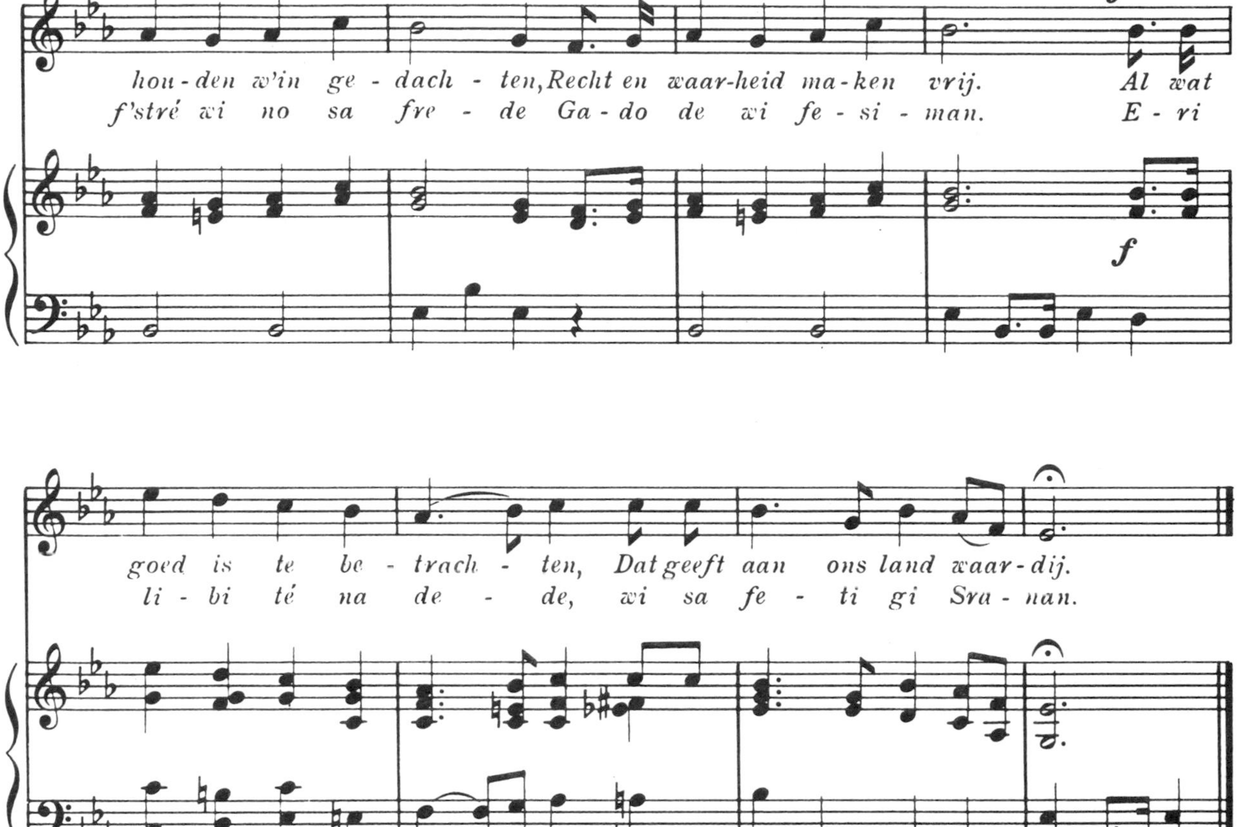

English translation of Dutch verse by
T. M. CARTLEDGE

God be with our Surinam!
May He glorify our beautiful land!
However we came together here,
We are pledged to your soil.
As we work, let us remember
That justice and truth make us free.
Practising all that is good
Will make our country a worthy land.

SWAZILAND

Words by
Mrs. A.F.K. SIMELANE

Music by
DAVID RYCROFT

This anthem was selected from some 100 entries in a National Anthem competition, when Swaziland attained independence on 6th September 1968. The composer, Mr. David Rycroft, is a Lecturer in Bantu Languages at the University of London, and author of the first Swazi-English dictionary. His anthem was composed after ethnomusicological fieldwork in Swaziland and is a compromise between Swazi and Western music. The Swazi musical tradition is unusual in that there are no drums. The stress is on choral dance-songs, with intricate polyphony, rather than on the more usual rhythmic subtleties found elsewhere in Africa.

*'c' is a dental click consonant.

Free Translation

O God, bestower of the blessings of the Swazi;
We are thankful for all our good fortune,
We give praise and thanks for our King
And for our country, its hills and rivers.
Bless those in authority in Swaziland,
Thou alone art our Almighty One.
Give us wisdom without guile,
Establish us and strengthen us,
Thou Everlasting One.

Notes on Pronunciation

Vowels: There are five vowels: a, e, i, o and u. These are rendered 'pure', much as in Italian, i.e. roughly as 'ah', 'eh', 'ee', 'aw', 'oo'.

Consonants: Each consonant or consonant cluster belongs with the following vowel, not with the preceding one. Consonant clusters must be treated as single phonemes without being split up, e.g. *neh / tee / ntsah / bah* (Not *neh / teen / tsah–* or *teent / sah–*).

(1) *ng* has a 'silent g' as in Southern English 'singing' (not as in 'anger').

(2) *ngg* is as in English 'anger'.

(3) *hl* is a lateral fricative like Welsh double–L, as in 'Llanelly'.

(4) *dl* is the voiced counterpart of *hl*. (Roughly: French 'j' (as in 'measure') pronounced simultaneously with 'l'.)

(5) '*c*' is a dental click consonant– a purely suction sound produced by withdrawing the tongue-tip from the teeth (with simultaneous velar closure).
This sound is sometimes used by English speakers to express annoyance (represented by 'tch' or 'tut-tut'). In Swazi, the following vowel has a 'k'- like onset.

(6) *tsh* is like English 'ts' (not 'ch') plus slight aspiration.

(7) *k* is like English 'g'; *nk* is as in English 'anchor'; *kh* is like English 'k'.

SWEDEN

Du Gamla, Du Fria

Words by
RICHARD DYBECK
(1811-1877)

Folk melody
Arr. EDVIN KALLSTENIUS
(1881-1967)

Maestoso

mf

1. *Du gam - la, du fri - a, du fjäll - hö - ga Nord, du*
1. Thou an - cient, thou glo - rious, thou alp - crown - ed North, Where

tys - ta, du gläd - je - ri - ka skö - na! Jag
free - born and hap - py hearts are beat - ing! We

mp

häl - sar dig, vä - nas - te land___ up - på jord, Din
hail thee, thou fair - est of lands___ on the earth. Thy

First sung in 1844; its use as a National Anthem dates from 1880-1890.

2. *Du tronar på minnen från fornstora dar,*
Då ärat ditt namn flög över jorden.
Jag vet, att du är och du blir vad du var,
:|: Ack, jag vill leva, jag vill dö i Norden! :|:

2. How proudly we dwell on thy great deeds of yore,
What time thy name was famed in story;
Thy sons still are valiant and brave as before:
:|: In thee I'll live and die, thou land of glory! :|:

SWITZERLAND

Swiss Psalm

SCHWEIZERPSALM
Words by L WIDMER (1808-1867)
CANTIQUE SUISSE
Ch. CHATELANET

SALMO SVIZZERO
PSALM SVIZZER
J. A. BÜHLER

Music by
A. ZWYSSIG
(1808 -1854)
Harm. G. DORET

Solenne
mf sostenuto
Ger. 1. Trittst im Mor - gen - rot da - her, seh ich dich im
Fr. 1. Sur nos monts, quand le so - leil Annonce un bril -
It. 1. Quan - do bion - da au - ro - ra Il mat - tin c'in -
Rom.1. In l'au - ro - ra la da - man at cu - gnuo - scha
Eng.1. When the morn - ing skies grow red And o'er us their
mf sostenuto

Strah - len - meer, dich, du Hoch - er - ha - be - ner,
- lant ré - veil, Et pré - dit d'un plus beau jour
- do - ra L'al - ma mia t'a - do - ra,
bain l'u - man spiert e - tern do - mi - na - tur,
ra - diance shed, Thou, O Lord, ap - pear - eth

The music was composed by Father Alberik Zwyssig, a monk, who adapted it to Leonhard Widmer's words in 1841
This was declared the official National Anthem by the Federal Government in September 1961
for a trial period of three years, ending on 31st December 1964. This trial period has been prolonged
until further notice, pending consultations.

mf espressivo
Herr - li - cher! Wenn der Al - pen -
le re - tour, Les beau - tés de
re del ciel, Quan - do l'al - pe
tuot - pus - sant! Cur ils munts stra -
In their light. When the Alps glow
mf espressivo
-firn sich rö - - tet,
la pa - tri - - e
già ros - seg - - gia
-glü - schan su - - ra,
bright with splen - - dour,
cresc.
Be - tet, frei - e Schwei - zer, be - tet!
Par - lent á l'âme at - ten - dri - e;
A pre - ga - re al - lor t'at - teg - gia;
u - ra, li - ber Sviz - zer, u - ra.
Pray to God, to Him sur - ren - der,
cresc.

f poco più mosso
cresc. poco a
Eu - re from - me See - le ahnt, Eu - re from - me
Au ciel mon - tent plus joy - eux, Au ciel mon - tent
In fa - vor del pa - trio suol, In fa - vor del
Ti - a or - ma sain - ta ferm, Ti - a or - ma
For you feel and un - der - stand, For you feel and
f poco più mosso
cresc. poco a
poco
a tempo
See - le ahnt, Gott im heh - ren Va - ter - land,
plus joy - eux Les ac - cents d'un cœur pi - eux,
pa - trio suol Cit - ta - di - no, Dio lo vuol!
sain - ta ferm Dieu in tschêl, il Bap e - tern,
un - der - stand That He dwell - eth in this land,
poco
a tempo
f
sostenuto
Gott im heh - ren Va - - ter - land!
Les ac - cents é - mus d'un cœur pi - eux.
Cit - ta - di - no, Dio lo vuol!
Dieu in tschêl, il Bap e - tern.
That He dwell - - eth in this land.
f
sostenuto

GERMAN

2. *Kommst im Abendglühn daher,*
Find ich dich im Sternenheer,
Dich, du Menschenfreundlicher, Liebender!
In des Himmels lichten Räumen
Kann ich froh und selig träumen;
Denn die fromme Seele ahnt
Gott im hehren Vaterland.

3. *Ziehst im Nebelflor daher,*
Such ich dich im Wolkenmeer,
Dich, du Unergründlicher, Ewiger!
Aus dem grauen Luftgebilde
Bricht die Sonne klar und milde,
Und die fromme Seele ahnt
Gott im hehren Vaterland.

FRENCH

2. *Lorsqu'un doux rayon du soir*
Joue encor dans le bois noir,
Le coeur se sent plus heureux, près de Dieu.
Loin des vains bruits de la plaine,
L'âme en paix est plus sereine;
Au ciel montent plus joyeux
Les accents (émus) d'un cœur pieux.

3. *Lorsque dans la sombre nuit*
La foudre éclate avec bruit,
Notre cœur pressent encor le Dieu fort;
Dans l'orage et la détresse,
Il est notre forteresse.
Offrons-lui des cœurs pieux
Dieu nous bénira (du haut) des cieux.

ITALIAN

2. *Se di nubi un velo*
M'asconde il tuo cielo
Pel tuo raggio anelo, Dio d'amor!
Fuga o sole quei vapori,
E mi rendi i tuoi favori,
Di mia patria, deh pietà!
Brilla, Sol di verità!

ROMANSCH

2. *Eir la saira in splendur*
da las stailas i'l azur
tai chattain nus creatur, tuotpussant!
Cur cha'l firmamaint s'sclerescha
in nos cour fidanza crescha
Tia orma sainta ferm
Dieu in teschel, il Bap etern.

3. *Tu a nus nun est zoppà*
çur il tschêl in nuvlas sta,
Tu imperscrutabel spiert, tuotpussant!
Tschêl e terra T'obedeschan,
vent e nüvlas secundeschan.
Tia orma sainta ferm
Dieu in tschêl, il Bap etern.

ENGLISH

2. *In the sunset Thou art nigh*
And beyond the starry sky,
Thou, O loving Father, ever near.
When to Heav'n we are departing,
Joy and bliss Thou'lt be imparting
For we feel and understand
That Thou dwellest in this land.

3. *When dark clouds enshroud the hills*
And grey mist the valley fills
Yet, Thou art not hidden from Thy sons.
Pierce the gloom in which we cower
With Thy sunshine's cleansing power,
Then we'll feel and understand
That God dwelleth in this land.

SYRIA

Words by
KHALIL MARDAM BEY

Music by
AHMAD and MUHAMMAD FLAYFEL
Arr. by HENRY COLEMAN

Allegro moderato
Hu-ma-ta al-di-ya-ri 'al-ay-kum sal-am A-bat an tu-zal-la
al-nu-fu-su al-ki-ram 'A-run-u al-uru-ba-ti bay-tun ha-ram
Wa-'ar-shu al-shu-mu-si hi-man la yu-dham Ru-bu 'u al-sha-a-mi
bur-u-ju al-'al-ai Tu-ha-ki sa-ma-a bi-'al-i al-sa-nai

Adopted c. 1928

TRANSLATION

Defenders of the realm
Peace on you;
Our proud spirits will
Not be subdued.
The abode of Arabism,
A hallowed sanctuary;
The seat of the stars,
An inviolable preserve.

Syria's plains are
Towers in the heights,
Resembling the sky
Above the clouds.
A land resplendent
With brilliant suns,
Becoming another sky
Or almost a sky.

TANZANIA

Mungu Ibariki Afrika

Words by a group of Tanganyikans

Music by ENOCH SONTONGA*
Arr. by V. E. WEBSTER

Moderato
f
1. Mun-gu i-ba-ri-ki A-fri-ca
2. Mun-gu i-ba-ri-ki Tan-gan-yi-ka
f
Wa-ba-ri-ki Vion-go-zi wa-ke He-ki-ma U-mo-ja na
Du-mi-sha u-hu-ru na Umo-ja Wa-ke kwa Wa-u-me na
A-ma-ni Hi-zi ni ngao ze-tu
Wa-to-to Mun-gu I-ba-ri-ki

*By permission of Lovedale Press, Cape Province, South Africa

The words of this anthem are composed from the six prize-winning entries to the competition announced by the Minister of Education on 31st July 1961. It became the National Anthem when Tanganyika achieved independence on 9th December 1961 and was retained as a National Anthem when Tanzania was formed by the union of Tanganyika and Zanzibar 26th April 1964 The music is a shorter version of N'kosi Sikelel'i Africa

Official English Translation

1. God Bless Africa.
Bless its leaders.
Let Wisdom Unity and
Peace be the shield of
Africa and its people.

CHORUS Bless Africa
Bless Africa
Bless the children of Africa.

2. God Bless Tanzania.
Grant eternal Freedom and Unity
to its sons and daughters.
God Bless Tanganyika and its People.

CHORUS Bless Tanzania
Bless Tanzania
Bless the children of Tanzania.

THAILAND

Sanrasoen Phra Barami

Words by
H.R.H. Prince NARISARANUVADTIVONGS,
modified c. 1913 by
King RAMA VI (King VAJIRAVUDH)
Unofficial free translation

Music by
HUVITZEN

Andante maestoso
ff
Kha wo-ra put-ta chao Ao ma-no lae si-ra
Hail to our King! Bless-ings on our
krarn Nop-pra pu-mi barn bu-na-ya-di-rek
King! Hearts and heads we bow
pp
Ek bo-ro-ma cha-ka rin Pra sa-ya-min pra yot-sa ying
To Your Ma-jes-ty now, Of our loy-al-ty we

By permission of Department of Fine Arts of the Thai Government.
Adopted as National Anthem, 1934
The music was composed in 1872 foı King Rama V (King Chulalongkorn)
The original text was modified c. 1913 by King Rama V.
(King Vasiravudh).

mf
yong Yen si - ra pro pra bo - ri barn
sing. Hap - pi - ly we live
Pon pra - koon ta rakn sa
by the care you give
p
Buong pra - cha pen su - ka
Great pro - tec - tor,
ff
sarn Kor ban - darn ta pra song dai Chong sa - rit dang
hail to our King! May the years bring ful - fil - ment
wang wo - ra ha ru - tai Du - ja ta - wai chai cha - yo.
in ev - 'ry - thing. Bless - ings on our King!

TIBET

Words by
TRIJANG RINPOCHE

Based on a very old piece
of Tibetan sacred music

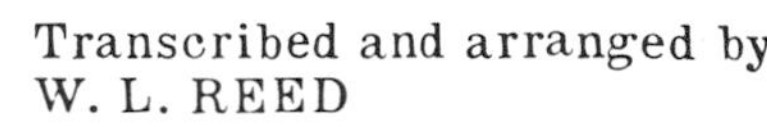
Transcribed and arranged by
W. L. REED

With dignity, but not too slow

f
Si - shi pen - de dö - gu jung - wi ter,
f

Tup - ten sam - pel nor - pu ö - nang bar. Ten - dro nor - dzin

gya - che kyong - wi gön Trin - lê kyi röl - sto gyê;

Dor - je kham - su ten - pê Cho - kün cham - tse kyong.

This anthem was composed by a group of scholars and officials who presented it to H. H. The Dalai Lama of Tibet in 1960. The words are by the Dalai Lama's tutor, Trijang Rinpoche. It is not used inside Tibet at the present time.

Nam - kö ga - wa gya - den u - pang gung - la reg.
Pün - tso_ de - shi nga - thang gyê. Pö - jong chöl - ka sum - gyi khyön - la
dzo - den de - kyi sar - pè khyap, Chö - si kyi
pel - yon tar. Tup - ten cho - chu gye - pê dzam - ling yan - pi kye - gu

shi - di — pe - la jor. Pö - jong ten - drö ge - tzen nyi - ö
kyi, Tra - shi ö - nang bum - du — tro - wi
zi, Na - cho mün - pi yu - le gye - gyur chi.

The source of temporal and spiritual wealth of joy and boundless benefits,
The Wish-fulfilling Jewel of the Buddha's Teaching, blazes forth radiant light,
The All-protecting Patron of the Doctrine and of all sentient beings
By his actions stretches forth his influence like an ocean;
By his eternal Vajra-nature
His compassion and loving care extend to beings everywhere.
May the celestially appointed Government of Gawa Gyaden achieve the heights of glory,
And increase its fourfold influence and prosperity.
May a golden age of joy and happiness spread once more through the three regions of Tibet,
And may its temporal and spiritual splendour shine again.
May the Buddha's Teaching spread in all the ten directions and lead all beings in the universe to glorious peace.
May the spiritual Sun of the Tibetan Faith and People,
Emitting countless rays of auspicious light,
Victoriously dispel the strife of darkness.

TOGO

Words by ALEX CASIMIR-DOSSEH
Trans. from French to Ewe by the
REV. FATHER H. KWAKUME

Music by
ALEX CASIMIR-DOSSEH
Arr. by HENRY COLEMAN

This National Anthem was chosen as a result of a competition between Togolese composers. It was first played on 27th April, 1960, the date on which Togo attained independence.

f più mosso
-blo - de koe ne - di. To - go, tsi - tre! Na -
vers la li - ber - té To - go, de - bout! Lut -
f più mosso
- wo̱ ka - lê nu - tsu - to̱e! Wo̱ a - wa nâ - du dzi a - lo na - ku bon! Ma - wu
- tons sans dé - fail - lan - ce Vain - quons ou mou - rons, mais dans la di - gni - té. Grand Dieu,
Gâ, Wo koe do mi de dzi. Ne To - go la na - no
Toi seul nous as ex - al - tés Du To - go pour la pros -
ff
ngo̱ yim la, To - go - vi, va! Mia - tu. De - nyi - gba la!
- pé - ri - té, To - go - lais, viens! Ba - tis - sons la Ci - té.
ff

EWE

2. *Miawo̱ do̱ ne le dekawo̱wo̱ me.*
Esia enye miafe dzime dzodzro vevieto̱
Naneke magbahe mo̱ na miafe nyatiatiaa o.
Miawo'si me ko ye wo dzo̱gbenyui kple wo ngo̱yiyi le.
Yata miade kluvi-ko̱kutiawo da
Anukwaredidi nano̱ mia me daa!
Mina miasubo̱ Denyigba la!
Togonyigba la nezu nami
Abe hehea fe Sikakpe ene.

FRENCH

2. *Dans l'unité nous voulons te servir*
C'est bien lá de nos coeurs le plus ardent désir
Clamons fort notre devise
Que rien ne peut ternir.
Seuls artisans de ton bonheur ainsi que de ton avenir,
Brisons partout les chaînes, la traîtrise
Et nons te jurons toujours fidélité
Et aimer, servir, se dépasser,
Faire encore de toi sans nous lasser
Togo Chéri, l'Or de l'Humanité.

English Translation

1. Hail to thee, land of our forefathers,
Thou who made them strong, peaceful and happy,
Men who for posterity cultivated virtue and bravery.
Even if tyrants shall come, thy heart yearns towards freedom.
Togo arise! Let us struggle without faltering.
Victory or death, but with dignity.
God almighty, Thou alone hast made Togo prosper.
People of Togo arise! Let us build the nation.

2. To serve thee in unity is the most burning desire of our hearts.
Let us shout aloud our motto
That nothing can tarnish.
We the only builders of thy happiness and of thy future,
Everywhere let us break chains and treachery,
And we swear to thee for ever faith, love, service, untiring zeal,
To make thee yet, beloved Togo, a golden example for humanity.

TONGA

Harmonised by
HENRY COLEMAN

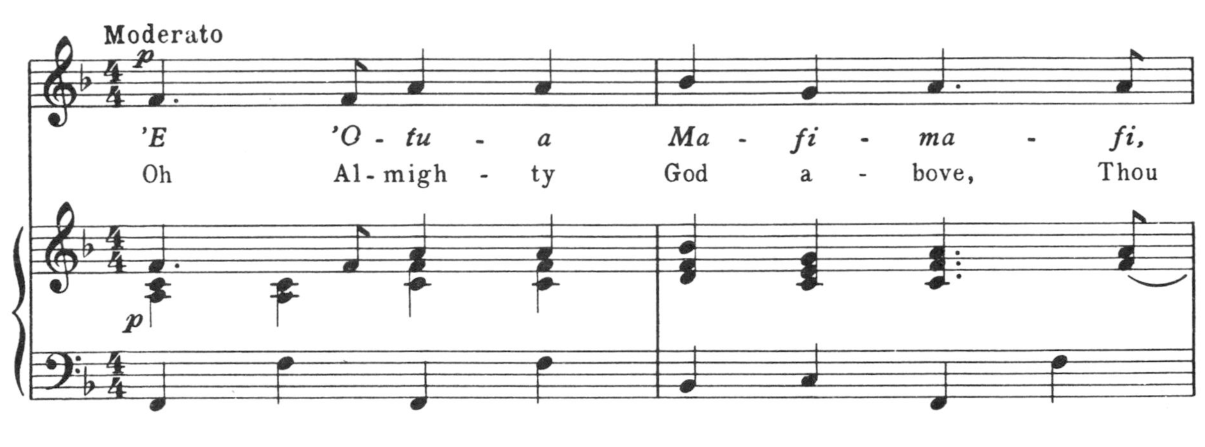
Moderato
p
'E 'O - tu - a Ma - fi - ma - fi,
Oh Al-migh - ty God a - bove, Thou
p

Ko ho mau 'Ei - mi ko - e, Ko Koe ko e
art our Lord and sure de-fence, In our good - ness

fa - la - la 'anga, Mo e 'of - a ki Tong - a:
we do trust Thee And our Ton - ga Thou dost love;

'A - fio hi - fo 'e - mau lo - tu
Hear our prayer, for though un - seen We
'Ai - a 'ok - u mau fai ni, Mo ke ta - li
know that Thou hast blessed our land; Grant our earn - est
mf
ho mau lo - to 'O ma - lu - 'i 'a Tu - pou.
sup - pli - ca - tion, Guard and save Tu - pou our Queen.
f

TRANSKEI

'Nkosi Sikelel'i Afrika

Words and Music by
ENOCH SONTONGA (died c. 1901)

This anthem has for many years been sung by the Bantu in central and southern Africa. By the Transkei Constitution Act of May 1963 it officially became the National Anthem of the Xhosa-speaking people of the Transkei.

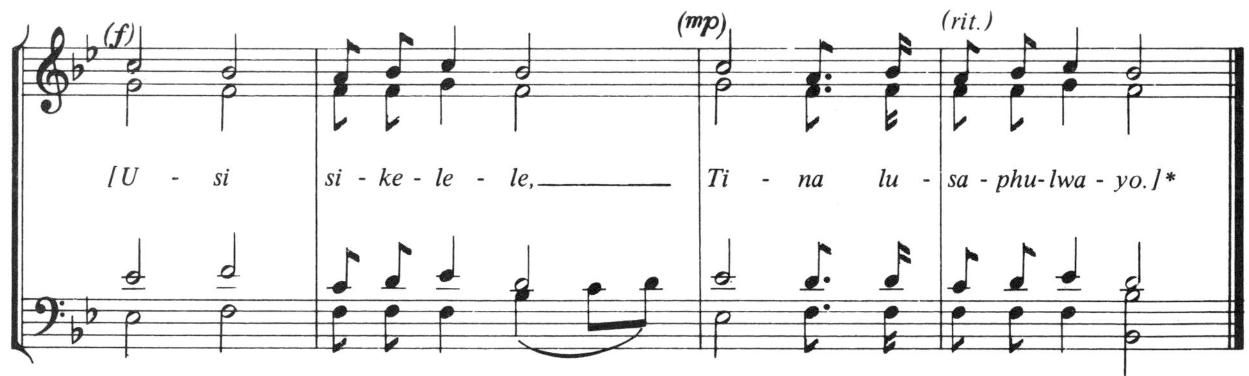

Free Translation

God bless Africa,
Let its banner be raised;
Hear our prayers and bless us.

Descend, O Spirit,
Descend, O Spirit,
Descend, O Holy Spirit.

* The words in brackets are not in the Transkei official version, but are in the version generally sung by the Bantu people. The national anthem of Tanzania, based on this melody, omits these last four bars of music.

TRENGGANU

Music by
CHE GU MOHAMED HASHIM BIN ABU BAKAR

Adopted in 1927 during the reign of the late Sultan Sulaiman Badrul Alan Shah.

Free Translation:

God save our King,
To reign over the State of Trengganu;
Peace and prosperity for their Majesties;
God save our King,
His subjects live in peace and security.

TRINIDAD AND TOBAGO

Words and Music by
PATRICK S. CASTAGNE (b. 1916)

Alla marcia moderato
mf
Forged from the love of
f
mf
8ves
li - ber-ty, in the fires of hope and prayer, With
rall.
bound-less faith in our des - ti-ny, we so-lemn-ly de - clare:
rall.

The National Anthem officially came into use at midnight on 31st August 1962 at the Flag Raising Ceremony held outside Parliament Buildings at Port of Spain, Trinidad. It was chosen as the result of a competition held by the Government.

Patrick Castagne is well known in the West Indies as composer, producer and broadcaster.

Published by permission of the Trinidad and Tobago High Commission, London.

Chorus
f a tempo
Side by side we stand, Is-lands of the blue Car-ib-bean Sea.
a tempo
8
ff
This our na-tive land, we pledge our lives to thee. Here ev-'ry
ff
creed and race find an e-qual place, And may God bless our na-tion. Here ev-'ry
allargando
creed and race find an e-qual place, And may God bless our na-tion.
allargando
8ves

TUNISIA

Words by
JALLAL EDDINE ENNAKACHE (b. 1912)
English translation by
Dr. ISMAIL HASSAN
Versification by
T. M. CARTLEDGE

Music by
SALAH EL MAHDI (b. 1925)
(Piano transcription by
T. M. CARTLEDGE)

Officially adopted 20th March 1958

HÄ-DUN TA-ḤAL-LÄ BI NAS-RIM-MU-BÎN ʻAL-ÄL GhA-SI-BÎN ʻAL-
fight is made sweet by a vic - to - ry sure Re - mov - ing the yoke we've
-ÄL ḤA - KI - MIN TU - GhÂT IZ - ZÄ - MÄN NÄ -
had to en - dure. The fire we con - front as
3
-KhU - DUL - LÄ HÎB BI RU - ḤIL HA - BIB ZA - ʻIM IL-WA-TAN
faith - ful we keep The spi - rit of our great lead - er Ha - bib.
Fine
Fine

VERSE
1. A - RAL ḤUK-MÄ LISh ShA - 'BI FÄN - BÛ LA - NA MI -
1. The peo - ple are sov - 'reign and so let us raise Of
-NÄL MÄDJ - DI A - 'LÄ SU - RÛ - ḤAN TU-ShÄD Ä -
glo - ry a cit - a - del for all to see. O
-DJÎ - BÛ Ä - DJÎ - BÛ LI' - AW - TA - NI - NÄ NI -
ans - wer, O ans - wer our fath - er - land's call To

-DÄ' - ÄL U-KhUW-WÄ-TI WÄL - IT - TI-ḤAD WÄ
true broth-er-hood and to true u - ni - ty. Be
ThÛ - DUL-'I-DÂ 'AN-HI-MÂ AR-DI-NÄ WÄ
rea - dy, like li - ons pre - pared for the fight, De -
CHORUS
KÛ - NÛ U-SÛ - DÄN BI-YÄW-MIL DJI-LÄD Ä -
-fend - ing our coun - try from each en - e - my. Im -

2. *WÄRITh①NÄL-JILÂDÄ WÄ MÄJDÄN-NIḌÂL*
WÄ FÎ ARḌINÂ MAṢRA ‘UL-GhÂṢIBÎN.
WÄ ṢÂLÄT ASÂṬÎLINÂ FIN-NIZÂL
TÄMÛJU BI ‘ABṬÂLINÄL-FÂTIḤÎN.
LIWÂ ‘UL-KIFÂḤI BIHÂTh②ÄSh-ShIMÂL
RÄFÄ-‘NÂHU YÄWMÄL-FIDÂ BIL-YÄMÎN.

3. *ShÄBÂBÄL-‘OLÂ ‘IZZUNÂ BIL-ḤIMÂ*
WÄ ‘IZZUL-ḤIMÂ BISh-ShÄBÂBIL-‘ÄTÎD.
LINÂ HIMMÄTUN ṬÂLÄTIL-‘ÄNJUMÂ
TU‘ÎDUL-MÄ ‘ÂLÎ WÄ TÄBNIL-JÄDÎD.
FÄḤÄYYUL-LIWÂ KhÂFIQÄN FIS-SÄMÂ
BI ‘IZZIN WÄ FÄKhRIN WÄ NAṢRIN MÄJÎD.

2. The glory and fight we inherit today.
Oppressors were fought here on this battleground.
Our legions in fury attacked in the field
As heroes in waves let their war-cries resound.
The banner of war in the North we have raised,
By oath we to ransom our land all are bound.

3. O noble the youth, our defence you assure,
Defending our honour, as ready you be.
Our strong aspirations reach up to the sky
That greatness return and a new day we see.
The flag, as it waves in the sky, now salute
With honour and glory and great victory.

Key to phonetic transliteration of Arabic text

^ for long vowels
Û as *oo* in *pool*
U nearer *u* in *put*
Ä as *a* in *cat*
A as *a* in *rather*
W at end of syllable as *oo*
*Th*① as *th* in *thing*
*Th*② as *th* in *this*
Ḥ aspirated at back of mouth
Kh like hard *ch* in German *Buch*
Gh like gutteral *r* in French *rang*
‘ like last *a* in *China*
Q̣ like *k* sound at back of mouth

TURKEY

Istıklâl Marsi

THE MARCH OF INDEPENDENCE

Words by
MEHMET AKIF ERSOY (1873-1936)
English versification by
T. M. CARTLEDGE

Music by
ZEKI ÜNGÖR (1880-1958)
Arr. by
T. M. CARTLEDGE

Pronunciation: ş like sh
c like j
ö and ü as in German.
ı (i without dot) more like final a of china

* lower notes optional for bass or alto voices.

Officially adapted as Turkey's National Anthem 12th March 1921

2. *Çatma kurban olayım çehreni ey nazlı hilâl*
Kahraman ırkıma bir gül ne bu şiddet bu celâl
Sana olmaz dökülen kanlarımız sonra helâl
Hakkıdır hakka tapan milletimin istiklâl.

2. Frown not, fair crescent, for I
Am ready e'en to die for thee.
Smile now upon my heroic nation, leave this anger,
lest the blood shed for thee unblessed be.
Freedom's the right of this my nation,
Yes, freedom for us who worship God and seek what's right.

UGANDA

Words by
GEORGE W. KAKOMA and PETER WYNGARD

Music by
GEORGE W. KAKOMA

With Dignity
mp
1. Oh U - gan - da! may God up - hold thee, We
lay our fu - ture in thy hand. U - ni - ted, free, For
cresc.
ff
lib - er - ty To - geth - er we'll al - ways stand.

2. Oh Uganda! the land of freedom.
Our love and labour we give,
And with neighbours all
At our country's call
In peace and friendship we'll live.

3. Oh Uganda! the land that feeds us
By sun and fertile soil grown.
For our own dear land,
We'll always stand:
The Pearl of Africa's Crown.

This National Anthem was selected through a competition, and came into use when Uganda became independent on 9th October, 1962. G.W. Kakoma is a Music Master employed in the Education Department, and P. Wyngard an English Master at Makerere University College.

UKRAINE

Words by
PAUL CHUBYNSKYI (1839-1884)

Music by
MICHAEL VERBYTSKYI (1815-1870)
Arr. by HENRY COLEMAN

Maestoso
mf
Con Ped.

f
Shche ne vmer - la U - kra-i - na, ni sla - va, ni vo - la,
f

Shche nam brat - tia mo - lo-di - i u - smikh-net'-sia do - la:

Performed as a choral work in 1864 in the Ukrainian Theatre in Lvov, it became officially recognised as the National Anthem in 1917, but is not at present used in that country where the U.S.S.R. anthem is officially used.

mf
cresc.
Zkhy - nut' na - shi vo - ro-zhen'-ky, yak ro - ssa na son - ci,
mf
cresc.
mf
cresc.
Allargando
Za - pa-nu - yem i my, brat-tia, u svo-ii sto - ron - ci,
mf
cresc.
Allargando
ff a tempo
Du - shu, ti - lo my po - lo - zhym za na-shu svo - bo - du
ff a tempo
I po-ka-zhem, shcho my, brat - tia, ko-zać-ko - ho ro - du.

English Translation

Ukraine has not died yet,
As freedom cannot die,
Be hopeful valiant brothers,
Our glory will revive.

Who us enslave, will perish,
As dew within sun's ray,
The enlightened rule of kin
Our country will regain.

Our soul and body willing
To give for liberty,
O, brothers, we are nearing
The path to victory.

UNION OF SOVIET SOCIALIST REPUBLICS

Words by
S. MIKHALKOV (b. 1913)
and EL-REGISTAN (b. 1924)*
Translated by
SOPHIE V. SATIN

Music by
A. V. ALEXANDROV
(1883-1946)

1. So - yuz ne - ru - shi - mi res - pub - lik svo -
bod - nikh Splo - ti - la na - ve - ki Ve - li - ka - ya Rus'. Da
zdrast - vu - yet soz - dan - ni vo - lei na - ro - dov, Ye -

Pronunciation: "Kh" = "Ch" in Scottish "loch"
"Zh" = "S" in English "measure",
' = palatalisation of preceding consonant

This became officially the Soviet National Anthem in 1943, replacing the "International".

*Words were slightly changed in 1977

di - ni mo - gu - chi So - vyet - ski So - yuz!
CHORUS
Sláv - sya, O - tye - chest - vo
f
3
na - she svo - bod - no - ye,
3

mf
cresc.
ff
Druzh - bi na - ro - dov na - dyozh - ni op - lot! Par - ti - a
Le - ni - na, si - la na - rod - nya - ya
1 & 2
Nas k tor - zhe - stvu Kom - mu - niz - ma vi - dyot! 2. Skvoz

2. *Skvoz' grozi siyalo nam solntse svobodi,*
I Lenin veliki nam put' ozaril:
Na pravoye delo on podnyal narodi,
Na trud i na podvigi nas vdokhnovil!

3. *V pobyedye bessmyertnykh idey Kommunizma*
Mi vidim gryadushchie nashey strani,
I krasnomu znamyeni slavnoi Otchizni
Mi budyem vsegda bezzavyetno verni!

Free Translation

1. Unbreakable Union of free-born Republics
Great Russia has welded for ever to stand.
Thy might was created by will of our peoples,
Now flourish in unity, great Soviet Land!

CHORUS Sing to our Motherland, home of the free,
Bulwark of peoples in brotherhood strong!
The Party of Lenin, the strength of our peoples,
To Communism's triumph lead us on!

2. Through tempests the sunrays of freedom have cheered us
Along the new path where great Lenin did lead.
To a righteous cause he raised up the peoples,
Inspired them to labour and heroic deeds.

CHORUS

3. In the victory of Communism's deathless ideals
We see the future of our dear Land,
And to her fluttering scarlet banner
Selflessly true we always shall stand!

CHORUS

UNITED ARAB EMIRATES

Music by
SAAD ABDUL-WAHAB

Arranged from the
Band score by
W. L. REED

(cresc.)
f

UNITED STATES OF AMERICA

The Star-Spangled Banner

Words by
FRANCIS SCOTT KEY (1779-1843)

Music by
J. STAFFORD SMITH
(1750-1836)

Words and Music officially designated as the National Anthem by Act of Congress approved by the President 3rd March 1931.

rock - ets' red glare, the bombs burst - ing in
air, Gave proof thro' the night that our
CHORUS
Poco meno mosso
f
flag was still there. O, say, does that
f
Star - Span - gled Ban - ner yet wave O'er the

2. On the shore, dimly seen thro' the mists of the deep,
Where the foe's haughty host in dread silence reposes,
What is that which the breeze, o'er the towering steep,
As it fitfully blows, half conceals, half discloses?
Now it catches the gleam of the morning's first beam,
In full glory reflected now shines on the stream;
'Tis the Star-Spangled Banner, O long may it wave
O'er the land of the free and the home of the brave.

3. O thus be it ever when free man shall stand
Between their loved homes and the war's desolation!
Blest with vict'ry and peace, may the heav'n-rescued land
Praise the Pow'r that hath made and preserved us a nation.
Then conquer we must, for our cause it is just,
And this be our motto: "In God is our trust."
And the Star-Spangled Banner in triumph shall wave
O'er the land of the free and the home of the brave.

UPPER VOLTA

Words and Music by
Abbé ROBERT OUÉDRAOGO
Arr. by HENRY COLEMAN

mf
1 Fiè - re Vol - ta de mes A - ïeux, Ton so - leil ar - dent et glo - ri - eux
mf
Te re - vêt d'or et de clar - té, O, Rei - ne dra - pée de lo - yau - té.
f CHORUS
Nous te fe - rons et plus forte et plus bel - le,
f

Approved as the National Anthem by the Upper Volta National Assembly on 3rd August 1960

ff
A ton a-mour, nous res-te-rons fi-dè-les, Et nos cœurs, vi-
ff
-brants de fier-té, Ac-cla-me-ront ta beau-té. -té.
1
D.C.
2

2. *Vers l'horizon lève les yeux,*
Frémis aux accents tumultueux
De tes fiers enfants tous dressés,
Promesse d'avenirs caressés.

3. *Le travail de ton sol brûlant*
Sans fin trempera les cœurs ardents,
Et les vertus de tes enfants
Le ceindront d'un diadème triomphant.

4. *Que Dieu te garde en sa bonté,*
Que du bonheur de ton sol aimé,
L'Amour des frères soit la clé,
Honneur, Unité et Liberté.

Free Translation by ELIZABETH P. COLEMAN

CHORUS We will make thee stronger and more beautiful,
We will stay faithful to thy love,
And our hearts, beating with pride,
Will acclaim thy beauty.

1. Proud Volta of my forefathers,
Thy glorious burning sun
Clothes thee in golden light,
O Queen draped in loyalty.

2. Raise thine eyes towards the future
Vibrating with tumultuous voices
Of thy proud children, standing ready,
The promise of a happy future.

3. The toil on thy burning soil
Will never cease to brace the fervent hearts
And the virtues of thy children
Will circle it with a triumphal crown.

4. May God protect thee in His goodness;
For the happiness of thy beloved land,
May brotherly love be the key
And honour, unity and liberty.

URUGUAY

Words by
FRANCISCO ESTEBAN ACUÑA de FIGUEROA (1791-1862)
English versification by
T. M. CARTLEDGE

Music by
FERNANDO QUIJANO (1805-1871)
and FRANCISCO J. DEBALLI (1793-1859)
Arr. by G. GRASSO

Officially adopted as the National Anthem by a government decree of 18th July 1845
The author was a poet and head of the National Library of Uruguay.

p
-tad o con glo-ria mo-rir! Es el vo-to que el al-ma pro-
-ty or with glo-ry to die! This the vow that our souls all have
p
-nun-cia y que he-ro-i-cos sa-bre-mos cum-plir, es el
tak-en And know how to ful-fil, cour-age high, This the
p
p
cresc. molto
vo-to que el al-ma pro-nun-cia y que he-
vow that our souls all have tak-en And know
cresc. molto
-roi-cos sa-bre-mos cum-plir, que sa-
how to ful-fil, cour-age high, to ful-
ff
ff

p
-bre - - mos cum - plir, es el
-fil, cour - age high, This the
p
cresc. molto
vo - to que el al - ma pro - nun - cia y que he -
vow that our souls all have tak - en And know
cresc. molto
ff
-roi - cos sa - bre - mos cum - plir, que sa -
how to ful - fil, cour - age high, to ful -
ff
-bre - - mos cum - plir,
-fil, cour - age high.

sa - bre - mos cum - plir, sa - bre - mos cum -
ful - fil, cour - age high, ful - fil, cour - age
- plir, sa - bre - mos cum - plir.
high, ful - fil, courage high.
Fine
Moderato
p VERSE
¡Li - ber - tad,! ¡li - ber - tad,! O - rien - ta - les Es - te
Li - ber - ty, Li - ber - ty, East - ern lands - men! 'Twas this
p
grí - to a la Pa - tria sal - vó! Que a sus bra - vos en fie - ras ba -
cry saved our coun - try of yore, And in - flam - ing its he - roes with
p
mf
p

1
2
p
mf
f
CHORUS
VERSE
-ta-llas, De en-tu-sias-mo su-bli-me in-fla-mó. ¡Li-ber-
pas-sion, Pre-pared them for fierce bat-tles' roar. Li-ber-
-mó. De es-te don sa-cro-san-to la glo-ria me-re-
roar. The glo-ry from this gift so sac-red We all
-ci-mos; Ti-ra-nos tem-blad! ¡Ti-ra-nos tem-
mer-it, A-way ty-ran-ny! A-way ty-ran-
-blad! Ti-ra-nos tem-blad! Ah! ¡Li-ber-
-ny! A-way, ty-ran-ny! Ah! Li-ber-

-tad en la lid cla - ma - re - - mos y mu -
-ty in the fight we shall cry for, And ex -
-rien - do tam - bién li - ber - tad!
-pir - ing still cry for li - ber - ty!
f CHORUS
¡Li - ber -
Li - ber -
f
Allegro
f
-tad en la lid cla - ma - re - mos y mu -
-ty in the fight we shall cry for And ex-
f
-rien - do tam-bién li-ber - tad! y mu -
-pir - ing still cry Li - ber - ty! And ex-

-rien - do tam-bien li-ber-tad!
-pir - ing, still cry Li-ber-ty!
ff
tam - bién li - ber - tad!
still cry Li - ber - ty!
ff
tam - bién li - ber - tad!
still cry Li - ber - ty!
dal 𝄋 al Fine
f
O - rien -
East - ern
f
dal 𝄋 al Fine

VATICAN CITY

Inno and Marcia Pontificale

Words by
ANTONIO ALLEGRA (1905-1969)

Music by
CHARLES GOUNOD (1818-1893)

Allegretto maestoso
Inno (Hymn)

f
Ro - ma im - mor-ta - le di Mar - ti - rie di
f

San - ti, Ro - ma im - mor-ta - le ac - co - gli i no - stri

can - ti: Glo - ria nei cie - li a Dio no - stro Si -
f

This became the official hymn in 1949. It is played (1) In the presence of the Holy Father. (2) In the presence of one of his Special Legates. (3) On the occasion of the presentation of Credential Letters by a Nuncio of the Holy See.

gno - re, Pa - ce ai Fe - de - li, di Cri - sto nel - l'a -
mf
mo - re. A Te ve - nia - mo, An - ge - li - co Pa -
p
cresc.
sto - re, In Te ve - dia - mo il mi - te Re - den -
dim.
p
cresc.
to - re, E - - re - de San - to di ve - ra e san - ta
f
dim.
p
cresc.

Fe - de; Con - - fo-rto e van - to a chi com - bat - te e
dim.
p
cresc.
cre - de, Non pre-var-ran - - no la
f
f
p
for - za ed il ter - ro - re, Ma re - gne -
cresc.
cresc.
ran - - no la Ve - ri tà, l'A - mo - re.
f
ff

f
ff
Sal - ve Sal - ve Ro - ma, pa - tria e - ter - na di me -
ff
mo - rie, Can - ta-no le tue glo - ri-e mil - le
pal - me e mil - le al - ta - - - ri. Ro - ma de-gli A-
ff
po - sto - li Ma - dre e gui-da dei Re - den - ti,

Ro - ma lu - ce del - le gen - - - ti, il mon - do spe - ra in
te!
Sal - ve Sal - ve Ro - ma, la tua
ff
lu - ce non tra - mon - ta, Vin - ce l'o - dio e
l'on - ta lo splen - dor di tua bel - tà.
ff

Ro - ma de-gli A-po - sto - li Ma-dre e gui-da dei Re - den - ti,
ff
Ro-ma lu-ce del-le gen - ti, il mon-do spe - ra in te!

English Translation

PONTIFICAL HYMN

O Rome immortal, city of martyrs and saints,
O immortal Rome, accept our praises.
Glory in the heavens to God our Lord
And peace to men who love Christ.

To you we come, angelic Pastor,
In you we see the gentle Redeemer.
You are the holy heir of our Faith
You are the comfort and the refuge of those who believe and fight.

Force and terror will not prevail
But truth and love will reign.

PONTIFICAL MARCH

Hail, O Rome,
Eternal abode of memories;
A thousand palms and a thousand altars
Sing your praises.

O city of the Apostles,
Mother and guide of the elect,
Light of the nations,
And hope of the world.

Hail, O Rome!
Your light will never fade;
The splendour of your beauty
Disperses hatred and shame.

O city of the Apostles
Mother and guide of the elect
Light of the nations,
And hope of the world.

VENEZUELA

Words by
VICENTE SALIAS
English versification
by T. M. CARTLEDGE

Music by
JUAN JOSÉ LANDAETA (c. 1780-1812)
Arr. by HENRY COLEMAN

Allegro marziale

f CHORUS

Gloria al bra - vo pue - blo que el yu - go len - zó, la
Glo - ry to the na - tion Who shook off the yoke, Yet

f

Ley res - pe - tan - do la vir - tud y ho - nor. - nor.
kept respect for Hon - our, Vir - tue and the Law. Law.

1 2

VERSE

mf

1. A -
1. "Let

mf

- ba - jo ca - de - nas! gri - tá - ba el Se - ñor; y el
loose all the chains, Let them van - ish", cried the Lord, And the

Adopted as National Anthem, 25th May 1881, by a government decree

mf
po-bre en su cho - za li-ber-tad pi - dó: A es - te san - to
poor man in his hov - el Li-ber-ty im - plored. At this ho - ly
mf
nom - bre tem-bló de pa - vor, el vil e - go - is - mo
name There trembled sore with fear The foul self - ish ty - rant,
f
que otra vez triun - fó. A es - te san - to nom - bre tem-bló de pa -
Who once triumphed here; At this ho - ly name There trembled sore with
f
poco rit.
- vor, el vil e - go - is - mo que otra vez triun - fó.
fear The foul self - ish ty - rant, Who once triumphed here,
poco rit.

2 *Gritemos con brío:*
Muera la opresión!
Compatriotas fieles
la fuerza es la unión:
y desde el Empireo
el Supremo Autor
un sublime aliento
al pueblo infundió.

CORO

3 *Unida con lazos*
que el cielo formó,
la América toda
existe en Nación;
y si el despotismo
levanta la voz
seguid el ejemplo
que Caracas dió.

CORO

2 Let's cry out aloud:
May oppression banished be!
Faithful countrymen, your strength
Lives in your unity.
And from highest heaven
The great Creater breathed;
A spirit sublime
Among us here bequeathed.

CHORUS

3 United by bonds
Made by heav'n's creative hand,
All America exists
As one united land.
And if tyranny
Should dare to raise its head,
Let all of us follow
Where Caracas has led.

CHORUS

THE SOCIALIST REPUBLIC OF VIETNAM

Words and Music by
VAN-CAO

Adopted as national anthem by the Provisional Government of the Democratic Republic of Vietnam from the first days of its formation, and by the National Assembly of Vietnam in its 2nd session in November 1946.
In July 1976 the first election of the United National Assembly of Vietnam adopted this national anthem for the whole country of Vietnam.

quang xây xác quân thù Thăng gian lao, cùng nhau lập chiến
lâu ta nuốt căm hờn Quyết hy sinh, đời ta tươi thắm
khu. Vì nhân dân chiến đấu không ngừng Tiến mau
hơn. Vì nhân dân chiến đấu không ngừng Tiến mau
ra sa trường. Tiến lên! Cùng tiến
ra sa trường. Tiến lên! Cùng tiến
lên! Nước non Việt-nam ta vững bền. Đoàn quân Việt-
lên! Nước non Việt-nam ta vững bền.
1
2
f
sf
8

French Version

1. Soldats vietnamiens, nous allons de l'avant,
Mus par une même volonté de sauver la patrie.
Nos pas redoublés sonnent sur la route longue et rude.
Notre drapeau, rouge du sang de la victoire, porte l'âme de la nation.
Le lointain grondement des canons rythme les accents de notre marche.
Le chemin de la gloire se pave de cadavres ennemis.
Triomphant des difficultés, ensemble, nous édifions nos bases de résistance.
Jurons de lutter sans répit pour la cause du peuple.
Courons vers le champ de bataille!
En avant! Tous ensemble, en avant!
Notre patrie vietnamienne est solide et durable.

2. Soldats vietnamiens, nous allons de l'avant,
L'étoile d'or au vent
Conduisant notre peuple et notre patrie hors de la misère et des souffrances.
Unissons nos efforts dans la lutte pour l'édification de la vie nouvelle.
Debout! d'un même élan, rompons nos fers!
Depuis si longtemps, nous avons contenu notre haine!
Soyons prêts à tous les sacrifices et notre vie sera radieuse.
Jurons de lutter sans répit pour la cause du peuple
Courons vers le champ de bataille!
En avant! Tous ensemble, en avant!
Notre patrie vietnamienne est solide et durable.

English Translation

1. Soldiers of Vietnam, we go forward,
With the one will to save our Fatherland,
Our hurried steps are sounding on the long and arduous road.
Our flag, red with the blood of victory, bears the spirit
of our country.
The distant rumbling of the guns mingles with our marching song.
The path to glory passes over the bodies of our foes.
Overcoming all hardships, together we build our resistance bases.
Ceaselessly for the people's cause we struggle,
Hastening to the battle-field!
Forward! All together advancing!
Our Vietnam is strong, eternal.

2. Soldiers of Vietnam, we go forward!
The gold star of our flag in the wind
Leading our people, our native land, out of misery and suffering.
Let us join our efforts in the fight for the building of a new life.
Let us stand up and break our chains.
For too long have we swallowed our hatred.
Let us keep ready for all sacrifices and our life will be radiant.
Ceaselessly for the people's cause we struggle,
Hastening to the battle-field!
Forward! All together advancing!
Our Vietnam is strong, eternal.

WALES

Hen Wlad fy Nhadau

LAND OF MY FATHERS

Welsh words by
EVAN JAMES
(1809-1893)
English Translation by
W. S. GWYNN WILLIAMS

Melody by
JAMES JAMES (1832-1902)
Arr. by W. S. GWYNN WILLIAMS

Moderato
mf
f
mf
Mae hen wlad fy nhad - au yn
The land of my fath - ers is

an nwyl i mi, Gwlad beirdd a chan - tor - ion, en - wog - ion o
dear un - to me, Old land where the min - strels are hon - oured and

fri; Ei gwr - ol ry - fel - wyr, gwlad - gar - wyr tra mâd, Tros
free; Its war - ring de - fen - ders so gal - lant and brave, For

CHORUS
f
rydd - id coll - as - ant eu gwaed. Gwlad, gwlad,
free - dom their life's blood they gave. Home, home,
f

This national song was first sung at the famous Llangollen Eisteddfod of 1858, and is now regarded as having the status of a National Anthem. It is also sung as a National Anthem in Brittany, to a Breton translation by Taldir.

pleid - iol wyf— i'm gwlad, Tra môr yn— fur i'r
true— am I—— to home, While seas se - cure the

bur hoff bau, O bydd - ed i'r hen-iaith bar - hau.
land so— pure, O may the old lan-guage en - dure.

2. *Hen Gymru fynyddig, paradwys y bardd,*
Pob dyffryn, pob clogwyn i'm golwg sydd hardd;
Trwy deimlad gwladgarol, mor swynol yw si
Ei nentydd, afonydd, i mi.

Gwlad, gwlad, etc.

3. *Os treisiodd y gelyn fy ngwlad tan ei droed,*
Mae hen iaith y Cymry mor fyw ag erioed;
Ni luddiwyd yr awen gan erchyll law brad,
Na thelyn berseiniol fy ngwlad.

Gwlad, gwlad, etc.

2. Old land of the mountains, the Eden of bards,
Each gorge and each valley a loveliness guards;
Through love of my country, charmed voices will be
Its streams, and its rivers, to me.

Home, home, etc.

3. Though foemen have trampled my land 'neath their feet,
The language of Cambria still knows no retreat;
The muse is not vanquished by traitor's fell hand,
Nor silenced the harp of my land.

Home, home, etc.

WESTERN SAMOA

The Banner of Freedom

Words and Music by
SAUNI I. KURESA (b.1904)
Arr. by HENRY COLEMAN

Moderato
f
Sa - moa, tu - la'i ma si - si ia lau fu'a, lou
pa - le le - a; Sa - moa, tu - la'i ma
si - si ia lau fu'a, lou pa - le - le - a;
ff
Va -
Pu -

On 1st January, 1962, Western Samoa became the first sovereign independent Polynesian State. This anthem was selected by the Council of the Committee to be the National Anthem and sung as the flag of the Samoan Government was raised.

- ai i na fe - tū o loo ua a - gia - gi - a ai; Le
le___ ma Tu - mu - a, I - tu 'au ma A - la - taua, A -
fa - ai - lo - ga lea o Ie - su na ma - liu ai mo Sa -
- i - ga i le Tai ma le Vaa o Fono - ti, Mā-lō Tau -
p
- moa Oi! Sa - moa e, u - u ma - u lau
- tai! Oi! Ma - lie toa ma Tu - pu - a, Le
ff
pu - le ia fa - a - va - va - u.
Ma - lo, ia fa - a - va - va - u.
'Au - a e te

Samoa, arise and raise your banner that is your crown.

Oh! see and behold the stars on the waving banner
They are a sign that Samoa is able to lead.

Oh! Samoa hold fast
Your freedom for ever.

Do not be afraid; as you are founded on God;
Our treasured precious liberty.
Samoa, arise and wave
Your banner that is your crown.

YEMEN ARAB REPUBLIC

Arranged by W. L. REED

No words

Tempo I°
ff

YEMEN

People's Republic of Yemen

No words

Music by
JUMA'A KHAN
Arranged by W. L. REED

First used on the occasion of the Independance of the People's Republic of Yemen, 30 November 1967.

YUGOSLAVIA

Words by
(1) JOVAN DJORDJEVIC (1826-1900)
(2) ANTUN MIHANOVIĆ (1796-1861)
(3) ŚIMÓN JENKO (1835-1869)
English words by LORRAINE NOEL FINLAY*

Music by
(1) DAVORIN JENKO (1835-1914)
(2) LICHTENEGGER (c. 1850)
(3) DAVORIN JENKO (1835-1914)
Arr. by HENRY COLEMAN

Andante maestoso

Bo - že — prav - de, — ti što — spa - se, Od pro - pa - sti
God of — jus - tice, — save thy — peo - ple, Lord, pro - tect us

do sad - nas, Čuj i — od sad - na - še — gla - se
day by — day; Hear our — voi - ces — sup - pli - cat - ing,

I od - sad nam bu - di - spas! Le - pa na - ša
Grant sal - va - tion now, we — pray. Bless - ed home - land,

This National Anthem is a combination, made in 1918, of the National Anthems of the Serbs, Croats and Slovenes. Part 1 is taken from the Serbian Anthem, Part 2 from the Croatian, Part 3 from the Slovene, and the last 4 bars from the Serbian. Music is sometimes attributed to Josip Runjanin.
The National Anthem "Hej Slaveni" is now officially used in Yugoslavia.

p
do-mo-vi - no, Oj ___ ju-nač - ka, zem - ljo mi - la.
we sa - lute thee, Fair - est proud soil, he - roes hold__ dear.
p
f
p
f
f
Sta - re sla - ve de-do-vi - no, da __ bi vaz-da čast-na bi - la. Na -
Fa - ther - land, al - legiance we pledge, Hon-our-ing__ thee, land without peer. "Ad -
f
p
f
f
Tempo marziale
- prej za - sta - va sla - ve, na boj ju-nač - ka kri. Za
- vance with ban - ners wav - ing! Fight on!" our he - roes cry. To
ff
bla - gar o - čet nja - ve naj pu - ška go - vo - ri! Na -
save our coun - try's glo - ry The roar - ing guns re - ply. "Ad -
ff

-prej za-sta-va, sla - ve, na boj, ju-nač-ka kri! Za
-vance with ban-ners wav - ing! Fight on!" our he-roes cry. To
bla-gar o-čet nja - ve naj pu-ška go-vo-ri!
save our coun-try's glo - ry The roar-ing guns re - ply.
f
Bo-že, spa-si, Bo-že, hra - ni, na-šeg Kra-lja i - naš rod!
God pro-tect our no-ble mon - arch, God watch o - ver great and small,
f
ff allarg.
Kra-lja Pe-tra, Bo-že, hra - ni, mo-li ti - se - sav naš rod!
God sus-tain and guide King Pe - ter, God de-fend and keep us all.
ff allarg.

YUGOSLAVIA

Hej Slaveni

Words Anon.

Traditional
Arr. by HENRY COLEMAN

Originally composed about the middle of the 19th century as an anthem of the Slavonic movement for the Union of Slavs and afterwards adopted by some of the Slavonic countries as their National Anthem. It became the National Anthem of Yugoslavia in 1945.

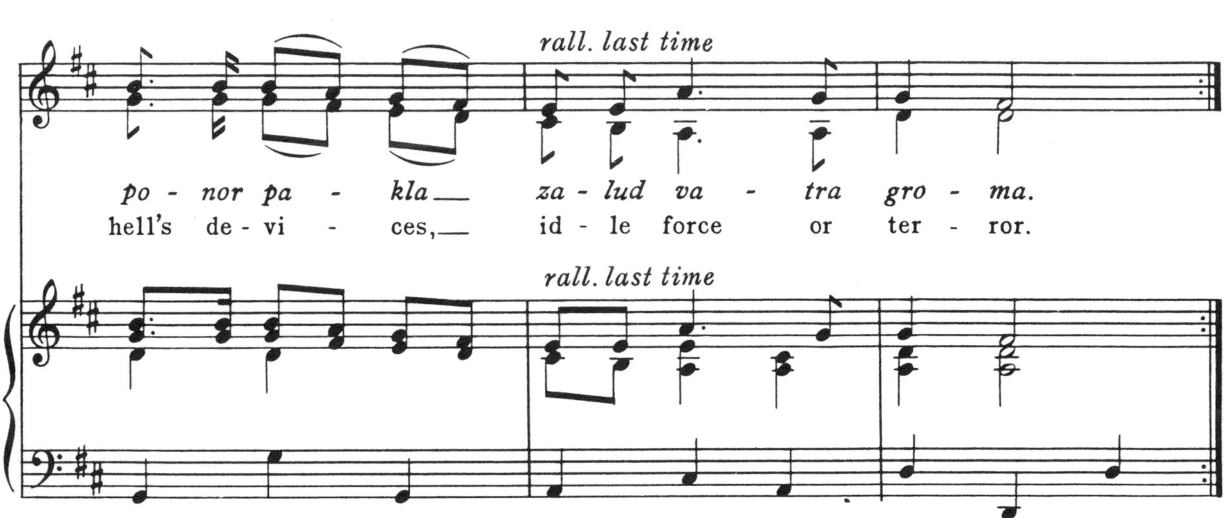

3 Let the tempest rage about us,
Sweeping all before it –
Rock is riven, oak uplifted,
Aye, the whole earth trembles,—

4 But we stand steadfast and constant
Like a granite mountain.
Curses be on all betrayers
False to our glad homeland!

REPUBLIC OF ZAÏRE

La Zaïroise

Words by
BOKA

Music by
LUTUMBA
Arr. by T. M. CARTLEDGE

Broadly and firmly
Za - ï - rois, dans la paix re - trou - vée, Peuple u -
- ni, nous som - mes Za - ï - rois. En a - vant, fier et plein de di - gni -

Adopted in 1971

-té,
Peu-ple grand, peu-ple libre à ja - mais.
Tri - co -
-lore, en flam-me nous du feu sa - cré
Pour bâ - tir no-tre pa-ys tou-jours plus
beau,
Au - tour d'un "Fleu - ve Ma - jes - té."
Au - tour
d'un "Fleu-ve Ma - jes - té."
Tri - co - lore au vent, ra - vi - ve l'i - dé -

-al Qui nous re - lie aux a-ïeux, à nos en - fants: PAIX, JUS-
-TICE et TRA - VAIL, PAIX, JUS-TICE et TRA - VAIL.

English translation

Zairians, in refound peace
We are a united people, Zairians.
Forward with pride and dignity,
A great people, for ever free!
O Tricolour, kindle the sacred fire in us
So that we may build our country finer yet,
Beside a "Kingly River",
Beside a "Kingly River".
Waving Tricolour, revive the ideal
Which binds us to our forbears and our children:
PEACE, JUSTICE and WORK,
PEACE, JUSTICE and WORK.

ZAMBIA

Music by ENOCH SONTONGA*
Arr. by Mrs. Walters and D. W. Dunn

With dignity
S
A
T
B
1. Stand and sing of Zam - bia, proud and free, Land of work and joy in u - ni - ty, Vic - tors in the strug - gle for the right, We have won free - dom's fight. All one, strong and free.
2. A - fri - ca is our own mo - ther - land, Fash - ion'd with and blessed by God's good hand, Let us all her peo - ple join as one, Bro - thers un - der the sun. All one, strong and free.
3. One land and one na - tion is our cry, Dig - ni - ty and peace 'neath Zam - bia's sky, Like our no - ble ea - gle in its flight, Zam - bia, praise to thee. All one, strong and free.
(S.T.) We've won
(T.B.) in the sun.
CHORUS – Sung after 3rd Verse only
(S.) Praise be to God. Bless our great na -
(A.T.) God. na -
(B.) Praise be, praise be, praise be, Zam - bia,

*The music for this National Anthem was originally written as a hymn tune at Lovedale Mission in Cape Province, South Africa. The tune became well known throughout a large part of southern, central and eastern Africa, and the words were translated into many African languages. Indeed, it came to be popularly known as the Bantu National Anthem. The tune was officially adopted by Tanganyika as its National Anthem on the achievement of Independence in 1961. New words have been specially written for Zambia. A competition was held and these words were produced as a composite version after a study of the ideas and the words of the six leading entries in the competition. By permission of Lovedale Press.

1. *Lumbanyeni Zambia, no kwanga,*
Ne cilumba twange tuumfwane,
Mpalume sha bulwi bwa cine,
Twaliilubula.
Twikatane bonse.

2. *Bonse tuli bana ba Africa,*
Uwasenaminwa na Lesa,
Nomba bonse twendele pamo,
Twaliilubula.
Twikatane bonse.

3. *Fwe lukuta lwa Zambia lonse,*
Twikatane tubyo mutende,
Pamo nga lubambe mu mulu,
Lumbanyeni Zambia.
Twikatane bonse.

CHORUS (after 3rd verse only)
Lumbanyeni,
Lesa, Lesa, wesu,
Apale calo,
Zambia, Zambia, Zambia.
Fwe bantungwa
Mu luunga lwa calo.
Lumbanyeni Zambia.
Twikatane bonse.

NATIONAL DAYS

AFGHANISTAN	27 May	*Independence Day, 1919*
ALBANIA	11 January	*National Day, 1946*
	29 November	*National Day, 1944*
ALGERIA	5 July	*Independence Day, 1962*
	1 November	*National Day, 1954*
ANDORRA	8 September	*Jungfrau von Meritxell Day (Patron Saint of Andorra)*
ARGENTINE	25 May	*National Day (Anniversary of May Revolution, 1810)*
	9 July	*Independence Day, 1816*
AUSTRALIA	26 January	*Australia Day, 1788*
	25 April	*Anzac Day, 1915*
AUSTRIA	15 May	*Signing of Austrian State Treaty, 1955*
	26 October	*National Day, 1955*
BARBADOS	30 November	*Independence Day, 1966*
BELGIUM	21 July	*Independence Day, 1831*
BENIN PEOPLE'S REPUBLIC	30 November	*Independence Day, 1975*
BOLIVIA	9 April	*Anniversary of the National Revolution, 1952*
	6 August	*Anniversary of Independence, 1825*
BOTSWANA	30 September	*Independence Day, 1966*
BRAZIL	7 September	*Independence Day, 1822*
BULGARIA	9 September	*National Day, 1944*
BURMA	4 January	*Independence Day, 1948*
	12 February	*Union Day, 1947*
BURUNDI	1 July	*Independence Day, 1962*
CAMEROON	1 January	*Independence Day,1960*
CANADA	1 July	*Canada Day (Anniversary of Confederation, 1867)*
CENTRAL AFRICAN EMPIRE	13 August	*Independence Day, 1960*
CHAD	11 August	*Independence Day, 1960*
CHILE	18 September	*Independence Day, 1810*
CHINA (Taiwan)	10 October	*Proclamation of Republic of Dr. Sun Yat-Sen, 1911*
CHINA (People's Rep. of)	1 October	*Proclamation of Provisional Constitution, 1949*
COLOMBIA	20 July	*Independence Day, 1810*
CONGO	15 August	*Independence Day, 1960*
COSTA RICA	15 September	*Independence Day, 1821*
CUBA	20 May	*Independence Day, 1902*
CZECHOSLOVAKIA	28 October	*Foundation of Czechoslovak Republic*
DENMARK	11 March	*Birthday of H.M. King Frederik IX, 1899*
	5 June	*Constitution Day, 1849*
DOMINICAN REPUBLIC	27 February	*Independence Day, 1844*
ECUADOR	10 August	*Independence Day, 1809*
EL SALVADOR	15 September	*Independence Day, 1821*
ENGLAND	23 April	*St. George's Day*
ETHIOPIA	1 September	*National Day, 1975*

FAROE ISLANDS	29 July	*National Day*
FIJI	20 October	*Independence Day, 1970*
FINLAND	6 December	*Independence Day, 1917*
FRANCE	14 July	*National Day (Bastille Day, 1789)*
GABON	17 August	*Independence Day, 1960*
GAMBIA, THE	18 February	*Independence Day, 1965*
GERMANY (West)	17 June	*Day of Unity*
GHANA	6 March	*Independence Day, 1957*
GREECE	25 March	*Independence Day, 1821*
GUATEMALA	15 September	*Independence Day, 1821*
GUINEA	2 October	*Proclamation of the Republic, 1958*
GUINEA-BISSAU	24 September	*National Day (Independence) 1974*
GUYANA	26 May	*Independence Day, 1966*
HAITI	1 January	*Independence Day, 1804*
HONDURAS	15 September	*Independence Day, 1821*
HUNGARY	4 April	*Anniversary of the Liberation, 1945*
ICELAND	17 June	*Anniversary of Establishment of the Republic, 1944*
	1 December	*Independence Day, 1918*
INDIA	26 January	*Republic Day, 1950*
	15 August	*Independence Day, 1947*
INDONESIA	17 August	*Independence Day, 1945*
IRAN	5 August	*Constitution Day*
	26 October	*Birthday of H.I.M. Mohammed Reza Shah Pahlevi, 1919*
IRAQ	14 July	*National Day*
IRISH REPUBLIC	17 March	*St. Patrick's Day*
ISRAEL	15 May	*Independence Day, 1948*
ITALY	2 June	*Anniversary of Proclamation of the Republic, 1946*
IVORY COAST	7 August	*Independence Day, 1960*
JAMAICA	6 August	*Independence Day, 1962*
JAPAN	3 May	*Constitution Day*
	3 November	*Cultural Day*
JORDAN	25 May	*Independence Day, 1946*
KENYA	12 December	*Independence Day and Republic Day, 1963 and 1964*
KOREA (South)	3 October	*Independence Day, 1948*
KUWAIT	19 June	*National Day, 1961*
LAOS	11 May	*National Day (Constitution Day), 1947*
	19 July	*Independence Day, 1946*
LEBANON	22 November	*Independence Day, 1943*
LESOTHO	4 October	*Independence Day, 1966*
LIBERIA	26 July	*Independence Day, 1847*
LIBYA	24 December	*Independence Day, 1951*
LIECHTENSTEIN	16 August	*Birthday of H.S.H. Prince Franz-Josef II, 1906*
LUXEMBOURG	23 June	*National Day*
MALAGASY REPBULIC	26 June	*Proclamation of Independence of the Malagasy Republic, 1960*
MALAWI	6 July	*Independence Day and Republic Day, 1964 and 1966*
MALAYSIA	31 August	*Malaysia Day*
MALDIVE ISLANDS	26 July	*Independence Day, 1965*
MALI	22 September	*Independence Day, 1960*
MALTA	8 September	*National Day, 1565 and 1940/3*

MAURITANIA	28 November	*Independence Day, 1960*
MEXICO	16 September	*National Day, 1810*
MONACO	19 November	*National Day*
MONGOLIA	11 July	*National Day, 1921*
MOROCCO	7 March	*Independence Day, 1956*
MOZAMBIQUE	25 June	*Independence Day, 1975*
NEPAL	18 February	*National Day, 1952*
NETHERLANDS	30 April	*Birthday of H.M. Queen Juliana, 1909*
NEW ZEALAND	6 February	*New Zealand Day, 1840*
	25 April	*Anzac Day, 1915*
NICARAGUA	15 September	*Independence Day, 1821*
NIGER	3 August	*Independence Day, 1960*
	18 December	*National Day*
NIGERIA	1 October	*Independence Day, 1960*
NORWAY	17 May	*Constitution Day, 1814*
OMAN	18 July	*Oman Day*
PAKISTAN	23 March	*Republic Day, 1956*
	14 August	*Independence Day,1947*
PANAMA	3 November	*Independence Day, 1903*
PAPUA NEW GUINEA	16 September	*Independence Day, 1975*
PARAGUAY	14 May	*Independence Day, 1811*
	25 November	*Constitution Day, 1870*
PERU	28 July	*Independence Day, 1821*
PHILIPPINES, THE	4 July	*Independence Day, 1946*
POLAND	22 July	*Constitution Day, 1952*
PORTUGAL	10 June	*National Day*
ROMANIA	9 May	*National Independence Day, 1877*
	23 August	*Anniversary of the Liberation, 1944*
RWANDA	1 July	*Independence Day, 1962*
SAN MARINO	3 September	*National Day*
SAUDI ARABIA	20 May	*Independence Day, 1927*
	23 September	*National Day, 1964*
SCOTLAND	30 November	*St. Andrew's Day*
SENEGAL	4 April	*Independence Day, 1960*
SIERRA LEONE	27 April	*Independence Day, 1960*
SINGAPORE	9 August	*Independence Day, 1965*
SOMALI	1 July	*Independence Day, 1960*
SOUTH AFRICA	31 May	*Republic Day, 1961*
SPAIN	2 May	*Independence Day,*
	18 July	*Labour Day (celebrated as Spanish National Day),1936*
SRI LANKA	4 February	*Independence Day, 1948*
SUDAN	1 January	*Independence Day, 1956*
SWAZILAND	6 September	*Independence Day, 1948*
SWEDEN	6 June	*National Day, 1809*
SWITZERLAND	1 August	*Anniversary of the Foundation of Confederation, 1291*
SYRIA	17 April	*National Day, 1943*
TANZANIA	26 April	*Tanzanian Union Day, 1964*
	9 December	*Independence Day and Republic Day, 1961 and 1962*
THAILAND	5 December	*National Day*
TOGO	27 April	*Independence Day, 1960*
TRANSKEI	26 October	*Independence Day, 1976*

TRINIDAD AND TOBAGO	31 August	*National Day, 1962*
TUNISIA	1 June	*National Day*
	25 July	*Anniversary of Proclamation of the Republic, 1957*
TURKEY	29 October	*Proclamation of the Republic, 1923*
UGANDA	9 October	*Independence Day, 1962*
UNION OF SOVIET SOCIALIST REPUBLICS	7 November	*Anniversary of the October Socialist Revolution, 1917*
UNITED ARAB REPUBLIC	23 July	*Anniversary of the Revolution, 1952*
UNITED STATES OF AMERICA	4 July	*Independence Day, 1776*
	27 November	*Thanksgiving Day, 1621. (This is celebrated the Fourth Thursday of November each year)*
UPPER VOLTA	5 August	*Independence Day, 1960*
	11 December	*National Day*
URUGUAY	25 August	*Independence Day, 1825*
VENEZUELA	5 July	*National Day. (Signing of Independence, 1811)*
VIET-NAM	1 November	*National Day, 1963*
WALES	1 March	*St. David's Day*
WESTERN SAMOA	1 January	*Independence Day, 1962*
YEMEN ARAB REPUBLIC	26 September	*National Day*
YEMEN (People's Rep. of)	30 November	*Independence Day, 1967*
YUGOSLAVIA	29 November	*National Day*
ZAÏRE	30 June	*Independence Day, 1960*
ZAMBIA	24 October	*Independence Day, 1964*